PENGUIN BOOKS

A YEAR IN THE WOODS

Colin Elford is a forest-ranger on the Dorset/Wiltshire border.

A Year in the Woods

The Diary of a Forest Ranger

COLIN ELFORD

With a Preamble by Craig Taylor

PENGUIN BOOKS

PENGUIN BOOKS

Published by the Penguin Group
Penguin Books Ltd, 80 Strand, London WC2R 0RL, England
Penguin Group (USA) Inc., 375 Hudson Street, New York, New York 10014, USA
Penguin Group (Canada), 90 Eglinton Avenue East, Suite 700, Toronto, Ontario, Canada M4P 2Y3
(a division of Pearson Penguin Canada Inc.)
Penguin Ireland, 25 St Stephen's Green, Dublin 2, Ireland (a division of Penguin Books Ltd)
Penguin Group (Australia), 250 Camberwell Road, Camberwell, Victoria 3124, Australia
(a division of Pearson Australia Group Pty Ltd)
Penguin Books India Pvt Ltd, 11 Community Centre, Panchsheel Park, New Delhi – 110 017, India
Penguin Group (NZ), 67 Apollo Drive, Rosedale, Auckland 0632, New Zealand
(a division of Pearson New Zealand Ltd)
Penguin Books (South Africa) (Pty) Ltd, 24 Sturdee Avenue, Rosebank,
Johannesburg 2196, South Africa

Penguin Books Ltd, Registered Offices: 80 Strand, London WC2R 0RL, England

www.penguin.com

First published by Hamish Hamilton 2010
Published in Penguin Books 2011

009

Preamble copyright © Craig Taylor, 2010
Text copyright © Colin Elford, 2010
Illustrations copyright © David Holmes, 2010
All rights reserved

Typeset by Palimpsest Book Production Limited, Falkirk, Stirlingshire
Printed in Great Britain by Clays Ltd, St Ives plc

ISBN: 978-0-141-04318-0

www.greenpenguin.co.uk

To my parents, Sheila and Paul Elford

'Colin would do well to keep his eyes
on the blackboard rather than on the
squirrels outside the windows!'

Class teacher, County Junior School Report, July 1966

Contents

Preamble   xi
Glossary   xviii

January   1
February   19
March   39
April   51
May   71
June   91
July   103
August   119
September   129
October   137
November   149
December   161

Acknowledgements   168

Preamble

One day a few weeks ago, Colin Elford travelled into London from Dorset and I spent a couple of hours with him talking about trees, forests and fallow deer. He doesn't often dress up but on that day he wore a green tweed jacket. It was bought for his eldest daughter's wedding but he was ordered to wear something a little more staid to that event, so it was only the second time he'd plucked it from his closet: the first occasion was a drinks party at his village hall. Usually Colin can be found at his place of work, which might broadly be defined as the woods stretching up into north and east Dorset and out into south-east Wiltshire. During one working day he might tramp through part of a four-thousand-hectare chunk of woodland. Another day he might work a seventy-hectare block of conifer forest ringed by hardwoods. Each of the areas of woodland has its own name, from Stonedown to Stoney Bottom, my own personal favourite being Vernditch, an old ditch covered in bracken and fern that lies between the villages of Broad Chalke and Martin.

On official Forestry Commission documents Colin's job title is 'Wildlife Ranger'. His responsibilities, in addition

to deer management, include inspecting fences, checking
for rabbits, trapping and shooting squirrels, clearing ponds
and maintaining dormice boxes. When he is out in the
woods stalking deer in the summer months he wears a
light loden jacket. In colder weather he favours moleskin
trousers and a camouflage deerhunter. Most people who
wear Barbour jackets or waterproof wax coats make a
rustling noise when they move. Silence is important for
Colin as he slips past brambles and broken ash limbs,
keeping out of the direct sun and weaving in and out of
the dappled shade. When he is stalking deer he takes note
of the wind direction to ensure his scent doesn't travel to
the wrong nostrils. He usually walks the forest alone.

Colin stalks in wellies with neoprene inserts. He walks
in wellies and drives in wellies. 'I live in wellies,' he once
told me. He swears by his thermal vest and if the day is
bitterly cold he sometimes wears one of the two balaclavas
his mother knitted for him a couple of years ago. They
look silly, he admits, but are essential for anyone who has
to spend hours in the cold, sitting fifteen feet above the
forest floor in a high seat used to watch for deer. There
are wintry days when the woodcocks float above and the
ravens flap and he hears the pigeons close by. Sometimes
owls come and sit near the seat, eager to observe a stranger
in their midst. Depending on the day, Colin uses either
his own Austrian rifle or a weatherproof German .243
calibre, provided by his employers. It's completely black

with plastic stock, as wood stock tends to swell after prolonged use in pouring rain. When it does continuously rain he sits in his high chair, cold and still and wet, as the wind rushes around him and the cool drops of water plink incessantly on the back of his neck while he tries to breathe calmly and watch the forest line for deer-like shapes. Those, he says, are the worst days for a deerstalker.

Some of the best days come in autumn when the leaf cover is blown. There's nothing better, he says, than getting up in the dark of a hard frost. There might be a cold wind pushing through the forest but it knocks the leaves off and Colin enjoys watching them flutter to the floor. Blustery wet weather does not make for good stalking, but it is exciting to listen to the sounds the forest throws up when the trees bend and the grunts and groans of the fallow buck resonate through the woods.

Colin started his career in forestry in 1970 when he was seventeen. His father didn't have a car at the time so his mother drove him to Charborough Park, a large estate in Dorset, to see the forester. He was the old type of forester, a man who won respect by never ordering a task to be done that he couldn't do himself. 'These guys were brown as berries,' Colin told me. 'They were fit from all that work. They had hard muscles and little patience. If you showed up five minutes late they were gone. There I was, small and straight out of school. My hands got blistered immediately and I would come home from each

day, fall asleep in my clothes and sleep until morning.'
The forester told him to come back in a year's time when
he had grown, so Colin worked roofing houses in the
Bournemouth area and reappeared in the forest a year
later with a little more muscle and a head of long hair.
'The forester asked me to cut my hair so it wouldn't get
caught in a machine we used called a peeler,' Colin said.
'But I think he just wanted me to cut my hair.'

Colin is now fifty-three. At five foot seven he's not
massive. Stocky, perhaps, but not fat, he says, certainly
not with all the walking he does. He can still fell and plant
like a trained woodsman but his hands are softer than they
have been in the past. Years ago, when he and the other
men were working the forest with long-handled hooks
called slashers, his hands became calloused, cracked from
the wood resin and rough from dragging rusty chains
through mud. Colin was always self-conscious about them
when he handed over money for a pint at the pub. Sometimes he'd ask his wife to go to the bar instead.

When it comes to the forests of Dorset there is no fixed
number for the amount of deer that need to be culled
each year. Instead, Colin takes his cues from the land and,
while conducting a survey, checks whether the smaller
trees are browsed by hungry deer mouths, whether the
butterflies are plentiful and the brambles are growing.
'People get hung up on figures,' he said. 'If the habitat
starts to look like a lawn I know to put the cull up. There

is never just a simple number. I'm not keen to shoot to kill.' But he does know how to follow a deer in his rifle sight, he knows how to shoot, and he can recognize the bubbly pinkish lung blood that leaks from a startled animal if his aim is true. He knows that a sure sign of an amateur is when a hunter aims for the deer's head. After working with the animals for thirty-six years and culling for thirty-four, when he finds food in the mouth of a just-culled deer he knows to be pleased the animal didn't see the end coming, the shot was quick, and the job done well.

When he writes about the forest, Colin uses an A4 notebook with the phases of the moon printed on the pages. He writes in pen. Years ago he was offered a Dictaphone but decided his voice sounded a little too weird, a little too much like Worzel Gummidge, when he whispered into a recorder in the dark. Instead he holds details – cream veins on an ivy leaf – in his head until he gets a pen in hand. At home, after bathing and checking for ticks, especially under his watch strap, he sits down in front of an old second-hand Forestry Commission computer and tries to write a page a night. He has to be in the right mood, and not too tired. Sometimes his wife leans over and says to him: 'Put a full stop there.' Colin has been married to Nicola for thirty-three years. She knew from the beginning, when they met aged sixteen, what life would be like with a forest ranger. A romantic night out with Colin tends to involve an activity such as badger watching. He could, theoretically, lie on a beach while on holiday, but he wouldn't last long. He can't turn off from thinking about the wildlife in his woods.

Colin is talkative. Sometimes when I speak to him on the phone an hour passes easily and he inevitably throws a detail into conversation that makes me miss standing under a canopy of trees. He has Stoney Bottom; here, in the city, the best I can do is seek out the weak imitative of a tree-lined street or a manicured park. Though he has no problem keeping up conversation Colin doesn't seek out companionship on the job. 'I'm not a loner but I prefer to be alone. I find it hard working every day with somebody,' he said during one phone conversation, and then he paused. 'Oh, look at that,' he finally continued. 'I'm just watching a buzzard out my kitchen window. He's displaying. That's an interesting sight.'

On the day of his London trip I asked Colin why forests mean so much to him. 'I could never have enough of being in the forest,' he replied. 'I love it so much. Each forest, even the urban ones, has a feeling or a vibe. Forests have moods. Only once have I been in one and felt like I had to leave. That was the power of that forest's mood. One night, in a field, I shot two deer and I had to drag them about a mile to the truck. I'm not scared of the dark but the ash trees were cracking above in the wind, the will o' the wisp – the ground fog – went whooshing past. A fox barked. I remember the glow over the trees.'

It was the one time he felt he was being watched and it set him on edge. Usually the forest has the opposite effect, calming him and filling him with a sense of belonging. 'As a boy, if I was ever upset, I loved to go out to the woods,' he said. 'It made me feel better. I can't say exactly what attracts me to a forest. On a lovely day, or one that starts with a cold frost, I still think, I've got to get out there.'

Craig Taylor

Glossary

beating up   replacement of trees that have died
shortly after planting

brashing   removal of lower branches from
the base of a tree (in forestry up to
two metres)

browsing   eating of buds and young tree
shoots

bumping   disturbing or surprising a deer
from cover

buttalo   small soft plastic device, which
when squeezed mimics the call of
a doe on heat or fear-stricken
young deer

call   attract male deer at the mating
season by various methods,
including 'deer calls', wooden or

plastic instruments, which when blown through imitate various calls of deer; and a 'beech leaf call', produced by blowing on a beech leaf held on edge and stretched between forefinger and thumb, which imitates the pheep of a roe deer

canopy   roof of the forest, formed by the crowns of the tallest trees

clear fell   harvesting and regeneration method that removes all trees within a given area

coppice   management based on regeneration by regrowth of cut stumps (coppice stools)

corvids   birds belonging to the family Corvidae, i.e., crow, raven, rook, jackdaw, magpie, jay and chough

cover   vegetative shelter for wildlife from predators and inclement weather

cull	management of deer numbers by controlled shooting
emparked	kept within the boundaries of an enclosed area of land
fallow	species of deer
fraying	damage caused by deers' antlers on the bark of trees – usually to mark territory or remove unwanted velvet
glassing	focusing on an object through binoculars or a spotting scope
gralloching	removal of the stomach and other internal organs from a shot deer
hazel mock	group of hazel shoots from a single stem
high seat	raised, laddered structure made of wood or metal used to watch or shoot deer from; can be permanently fixed or portable

leader   forestry term for a year's lateral
                        (top) growth on a tree

lop and top   unproductive woody debris left
                        over from a cutting operation

mire   year-round waterlogged shallow
                        peat area of low-lying ground

natural regeneration young seedlings that have arisen
                        from seed falling near by

overstood hazel   hazel taken out of a rotation of
                        coppicing

pricket   male deer in his second year

pronking   stiff, strutting gait

rack   cleared track within a forest crop
                        used for timber extraction

restock site   re-establishing an area by planting,
                        generally following recent clear-fell
                        operations

ride   open track or break separating
                         plantations within the woodland

roding   displaying flight and croaking call
                         of a male woodcock

roe   species of deer

scrapes   lair or place where a deer 'beds' or,
                         in the case of fallow, 'lodges'

sika   species of deer

squirrel hopper   L-shaped tunnelled container
                         holding poisoned bait

stand   area constant in location used by
                         fallow deer (rutting stand)

thinning   tree-removal practice that reduces
                         tree density and competition in a
                         given area. The remaining trees
                         grow more vigorously; thinning
                         benefits wildlife by increasing
                         light values to the forest floor,
                         encouraging ground vegetation

torpid	state of torpor (moribund and inactive) as the body cools to a little above its surroundings
tush	anal hair tuft found on roe doe
unbrashed	lower unpruned branches of a tree (usually dry and dead)
understory	shrub layer below the forest canopy that receives little light
velvet	furry membrane covering growing antlers

January

It's early, and in the dark I stagger to find the door handle to the kitchen. A blast of wind and rain throws itself at the kitchen window. I peer out, tea in one hand, and stare into the darkness, judging the opposition.

Outside I point to the open door of my truck, and both dogs quiver in anticipation, waiting for my command. I say the word – 'Up' – and Kiesal, my Bavarian bloodhound cross, and Liv, the black Labrador, respond instantly, leaping eagerly into the vehicle. Over the years my truck has become a mobile kennel, office and portable deer larder. Within it I store and carry the everyday tools and equipment that I need: binoculars, shooting sticks, torches and knives, as well as the winch, a selection of pulleys and ropes, plus a rucksack for carrying smaller deer out of the forest. It is as natural for me to take my rifle to work as it is for a carpenter his hammer.

When I drive off there's plenty of debris on the road. Large fully leaved branches and small leafless sticks lie shattered, strewn on the smooth, dark, wet tarmac surface. Hand-sized leaves scatter as I pass over them, involuntarily drawn up to the headlights and cast away in the updraught.

As I unlock the barrier to the forest, I glance back at the truck. Spots of rain fall, caught in the headlights – the only light in the gloom. A pigeon flutters away in the dark as I shut the truck's door. I drive slowly up the track, deeper into the centre of the forest. Beyond the headlights it looks inhospitable outside and pelting rain smashes against the windscreen.

Picking the best time to leave between showers, I make my way to the high seat in this area of wood. I climb the sodden structure and sit quietly, surveying my view as the rear of my trousers sucks up the cold moisture from the bench seat. Up here, the owls are calling all around me. It's dark, real dark, ink dark. After misjudging my timing I have managed to get to the seat too early. In the forest there's no light, no colour. At this time of the morning there are merely shades, shades of blacks and lighter shades of greys, but no browns or greens, the natural colours of the forest.

The owls sound as though they're having a competition going on to see which one can make the loudest and longest hoot. Away in the distance I hear different calls, the screeching chatter of the blackbird. In the dark, opposite the high seat, another sound resonates; a sound like a lion crossed with a pig, a mixture of a roar and a grunt, as if the creature is continually trying to clear its throat. Only now is the dawn light starting to arrive. Will it ever get bright? It appears second by second like a sleepwalker slowly moving towards the light.

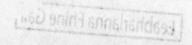

A sparrowhawk whooshes over my head, almost touching my hair. It jigs between the branches, oblivious of my presence, then sweeps down, making a sharp turn to the right, accelerating and disappearing up a very narrow and overgrown ride. I glance to my side and can just about make out the grapefruit yellow of the dying hazel leaves next to my elevated position. Only now is it possible to make out the shapes of the closest of the bushes and the underwood, dark greens against a darker surround.

The pine tops around the seat sway in the wind, their silhouette like a mountain range against the overcast milky-grey sky. I sit motionless, entranced by the colour and movement of the sky, my ears listening out for the sounds and calls around me. I mentally file the sounds away in my head, ticking off the noises I know and guessing at the others. There's the first call of the wren, so loud and strong yet melodic, while the blackbird still pipes away at a distance. All around me more birdsong, different voices with separate vocals and all at different levels. Sounds enclose me, and I hear the constant drumming of the water droplets sliding off a drenched leaf above, showering single-storey bushes below me. The stone-tapping alarm calls of the blackbird have stopped. It's also getting slightly easier to make out the shapes around me, though colour has yet to appear at distance. I stare at a close sodden leaf with a silvery sheen, dancing alone in the wind: the last to fall, its family gone, it waits its turn in nature.

The strange grunting is close now and I can make out movement: the shape of a lone fallow buck. I glass the shape: he's dark and trots oddly, carrying an injury possibly collected in the rut. Limping, he crosses the ride to my right, but he's too far away and too quick, and as I move my rifle scope over his mass there's far too much branch debris between him and me. It's definitely the right deer to take. Although injured it is moving fast, maybe too fast to stop. I call to it: 'Hey!' It halts momentarily, behind a tree, then moves on even faster. I cuss myself under my breath for not cutting the lower branches close to the seat, which now, water laden and heavy, bend and obscure my view. I cuss for not putting the maintenance in; it's certainly costing me now as it is possible I will never see that buck again.

Movement in front catches my eye, and my sight leaves the buck, for below the brow of a slope a dark fallow doe manoeuvres towards me, tense but fully alert, tuned in to her environment. Behind her, travelling in her footfall, are three more of the herd, all of various colours. Fingers of sunlight seek low over the forest floor as the deer slow at the timber edge before crossing the ride. The crosshairs of my rifle scope find the last and smallest of the herd – a doe. At the pause, I check she's broadside and that I have a clear backstop for the bullet. The rifle cracks, and waiting for the strike I watch her fall. The rest run off in a line to the safety of the thicket. Quiet returns and

I remain still, allowing the forest to become alive again. As I sit in my perch, the light finally arrives, flooding everything around me. It's going to be a lovely day. I sit and wait, listening to the calls of an annoyed jay.

I'm back again in the same seat, but this time I arrive a little later. The frozen truck tracks are uncomfortable to walk on and the leaves on the path lie curled and crisp, announcing my every step. I move more slowly than usual, trying to avoid hidden puddles of ice caught in the ridges of the vehicle tracks; if I miss my footing then the ice cracks loudly, making me wince and cuss. At least it's slightly lighter this morning, and the frost helps, with its sparkling illuminations on the path to my high seat.

I have almost reached the seat when a grey form passes me, looking as though it is floating across the frozen ground. No sound comes from the fox. It stops abruptly, as if it has walked into a brick wall, which in a sense it has as it picks up my scent that lingers on the ride edge. Turning sharply without giving a glance in my direction it leaves the area, manoeuvring itself over frozen obstacles silently. The seat looks like an ice sculpture this morning. At every rung my woollen mittens stick to the ice crystals that encrust the metal frame.

The light comes more quickly today; I have been in the seat for about twenty minutes when a movement to

my left catches my eye. Two chestnut tan-coloured fallow
does pronk, one behind the other, out of the shelter of
the hawthorn scrub into view under some well-spaced
beech. Throwing my binoculars to my eyes I select one.
It is an easy assessment for the first is scrawny and thin-
necked, her long nose a sure sign of age. The cross-hairs
of the scope soon find her. Taking a chance, for I know
they are committed to go somewhere only they know, I
call out to them. The shout ('Hey, you!') does the trick,
for both deer pause before crossing the ride, enabling me
to drop the selected female. As usual with true wild fallow
there is no time for mourning. At the shot the younger
doe speeds away without stopping, back to where the
pair first appeared from within the hawthorn thicket.

Manage to get soaked this morning, and tonight finds
me back once more in the same seat. The one with no
roof. And here comes the rain again.

When you control deer you spend many hours alone,
watching and waiting, but mainly waiting, usually in a
high seat. These come in various forms, providing different levels of comfort. The luxurious Thetford high seat,
for example, is a wood-clad tower with a roof supported
on four twelve- to fifteen-foot-long poles, which keeps
you, and more importantly your rifle and binoculars, dry.
Being square, the cabin offers four supportive shooting

points, allowing stability for a long shot and all-round visibility.

Having no such five-star seats on my beat I tend to use the less elaborate type, the lean-to, which is a seat on a ladder that can be leant into and wired on to almost any suitable tree. Placing one near a young plantation gives me a few years of use as the trees slowly mature, saving the need for constant moving.

Portable seats are my favourite choice; lightweight, they can be easily transported to any part of the forest. There are several designs: some come fully erected and can be carried on a roof rack; there is also a fold-up model, compact enough to fit in the boot of any mid-sized car.

More important than any of these designs, however, is getting the siting of the structure right in the first place, preferably at the end of a debris-free track, enabling you to stalk quietly through the woods to reach it.

With a damp fog getting thicker it is too dangerous to carry on stalking so I decide to call it a night and have another bash in the morning. Climbing back up the hill with the truck I am surprised when I drive out the other side of the cloud of fog, as if in a plane rising above the cloud line. I enter the plateau to a bright and miraculously sunny scene.

It is still snowing as I leave the house this morning. Not everyone likes snow, and I imagine in some areas of the country it must be a real nuisance. But, myself, I like the snow and I even find certain snows, freshly laid, absorbent and unfrozen, helpful in aiding me to get my cull.

When I drive out of my village the headlights reveal a different world to the one I went to bed in the previous night. But the truck is in its element and cuts through the morning's virgin snow like a wire through cheese. When the sun finally comes out I am welcomed by sights few others would see, still tucked away in the warmth of their blankets. The first crimson rays of the sun touching the powdered snow that coats the packed branches of the fir trees in the forest remind me of the beauty of an apple. The pleasure I get from such mornings makes me feel very lucky that I am in a position to see such incredible things. Surely your very soul needs to absorb such visions, which allow you to appreciate the nature around you. When occasionally I get low with the politics of life, I think what a privileged position I have with my office being the forest itself. At times like these I might think back to those sunny days when, on my travels from one forest block to another, I pass several small industrial units. Sat outside the units for maybe only a quarter of an hour, a small group of pasty-coloured factory workers will have congregated, attempting in their lunch break to catch a few rays of sunlight. They sit like grubs on a carcass with their faces turned skywards, feeling the glory of it and perhaps wondering where it all went wrong.

Today the ground is as hard as iron: a new world. I love this weather; it lets you know you're having a winter. I'm glad we sometimes get conditions like this; I think I'd miss the experience of getting into the truck when the seat feels like a solid lump, the moisture in the material of the seat having frozen hard. I leave early this morning even though the truck is putting up a protest, first refusing to start and then punishing me by not allowing any heat into the icy coffin of a cab.

Surprisingly this evening I account for three roe does despite the cold, catching them feeding on ivy on a wind-blown larch. The expired body-heat steam in the back of the truck does little to bring warmth into the icy cab. I have yet to feel my feet. That aside, my spirits are high. Outside, the stars are visible above me in the Milky Way, and patches of snow remain on the ground, waiting for fresh fall to join them up again. A massive, brilliant full moon lights up my path back to the last roe doe I culled. I savour the experience and the mood, for rather than feeling desolate the forest is welcoming. I banished all

fear of the night long ago, instead embracing it, thankful
that I can revere and appreciate all it has to offer.

While working today with a group of volunteers scrub-
cutting, we uncover the winter ground nest of a torpid
dormouse. The strange thing is the nest is right next to
an active badger run. Old brock's eyesight is not particularly good but he has got an amazing sense of smell, so I
am surprised the hazel mouse had not been snobbled up
for a snack. I guess a sleeping dormouse doesn't give off
very much, if any, scent. We decide to let nature take its
course, re-covering the nest with woodland materials and
leaving in situ. (On an inspection in the spring I notice
that the dormouse has made it through the winter, and
the nest is completely undisturbed. Phew.)

This afternoon a small falcon flies over the bonnet of
the truck, carrying a songbird in its talons, but it is not
a bird of prey I am familiar with. In the forest we have
resident buzzards, sparrowhawk and peregrine and, on
the heathland areas, the hobby. Later I identify the
stranger as a merlin, the smallest of all the falcons in
the British Isles. It was certainly swift and powerful for
its size, and cute.

Today I have a comical sighting of five male squirrels pursuing the scent of a single female. Wherever the female leads the males follow, in single file, chasing her, bewitched, up and down the trunk and across the moss-covered branches of an ancient oak. The female finally comes to the ground and the male suitors follow obediently in a line, making snuffling noises as though hoovering the ground, treading in her every footfall as a pack of bloodhounds would on the trail of a fox. I watch as she leads the lovesick males in a trance of lust back up the tree for another route march around the canopy. I wonder if they'll ever catch up with her.

It has been threatening to snow all morning and by early afternoon the flakes are rapidly covering the ground. When I leave to stalk for the rest of the afternoon only four-wheel-drives are still able to get up the hill – already a few two-wheel-drives have been abandoned. Because of cars blocking the road, and snowdrifts caused by the wind blowing through the open farm gateways, my route is hampered and it takes longer than usual to reach the wood. Opening the barrier I know I am entering an arctic world.

The freshly pitched snow, glinting like crystal glass, stretches pristine before me. There are no human foot-marks, no vehicle tracks. I have the wood to myself. The snowfall slows to small silvery gems and as I pause for a moment I am coated in winter's handiwork. Overhead a few struggling leaves cling desperately to branches, rattling dry and crisp, the cold wind battering and tearing at them. The bitter gusts make me shiver enough to have to do my top button up as they push and harass miniature snow twisters, brushing them along and off into the larger drifts. The sight is one of a white desert, but although it looks bleak, I feel warm inside. To encounter alone such weather in the failing pale afternoon light is sheer magic.

I follow a meandering ride, which takes me deep into this white kingdom. All around are animal and bird tracks. Stories are here to be read of life and death on the snow blanket: by this discarded cone a squirrel fed, and here a mouse cleared snow from the mouth of its hole. Further up the ride, feathers – fluffy and grey, once worn by a chaffinch and now half frozen in the stiff wind – twist and sway. Dotted about the scene, particles of red tell of an aerial hunt that ended on this lonely patch of snow. Taken in the air the songbird was cast to the ground, the weight of its pursuer leaving its body dent in the snow. The wing-tips marked the ground when it rose to the sky with its partially plucked prize.

I glass within the large expanses of bramble, looking for an unobservant roe doe, and am happily surprised how quiet and fast I can move in this type of snow. It absorbs the weight of my wellies and, being unfrozen, it feels and sounds like polystyrene, slightly squeaky if you walk too fast but ideal if you are prepared to take it slowly. In the sea of white I can easily pick out my quarry, but with the boot on the other foot my prey can just as easily spy on my movements. Stealth and hunting experience are the only things that can give you the edge. I know the deer will be extra hungry and, as the weather is set to last, with the temperature dropping, they will become uncomfortable, the cold making them rise earlier than usual.

Inside the bramble, under the canopy of the trees, the snow and wind have failed to cover everything with a blanket of white. After finding myself a bare patch, I spot a doe and her young busily blowing the dusty-textured snow off green shoots of bramble with short nasal blasts of air. The sound they make is not one I am familiar with – it's a low frequency, unlike the higher-pitched noise a roe often emits. Out of the darker shades and shadows of the crop trees further roe join the pair.

Down the ride, in the distance, I catch sight of two more shapes, in a field of perfect white, crossing the ride. Even though these deer are further away, the silhouettes they cast make them easy to sex, the anal tush sharp and clear on the canvas of snow. It is with a feeling of reluctance that I stop short a life in such a wonderful setting. But I play my part as predator and am punished by the trek back to the vehicle, having to carry the pair back in the same roe sack.

Picking my way home through the snow-covered countryside, I have time to reflect on the night's events and why it still leaves me with small pockets of regret.

Like a worn-out page that I have read over and over again, I understand the reasoning behind deer control. Kept at the right numbers, deer have a role to play in the ecology of the forest; they also provide immense enjoyment for the human soul when we see them in the wild. With our large predators gone, man sets his own agenda and dictates what he perceives to be the right number of deer allowed to survive. I'm certainly glad I'm past my youthful keenness for numbers and the bang-bang-buggery stage of my life that every hunter goes through, trying to impress the older guys, who quite rightly merely shrug in response, unimpressed. They are well aware that one day you too will lose that strong desire to kill, as sure in that knowledge as in the knowledge that a young caterpillar will grow to become a butterfly. If you can go stalking and feel no pain yourself when you take a life or wound an animal, then you are not fit for the purpose. It is healthy and indeed wise at times to examine the role you fill, while having a justified reason to end a life that you can explain to no one but yourself. The experiences I share with the deer in weather and places like these leave me with feelings of great respect and also a form of regret, and yet all these feelings combine to enforce a love for the whole system. I talk, sleep and eat deer – we are joined, a pair!

It's certainly not a perfect world, for why have we ticks? I have been flat out on the roe doe cull, so every night before having a bath I have got into the routine of a tick check. While washing my mop I notice and feel a pair of unwelcome visitors climbing around in my hair. Deer lice can be a real pain to grab, you chase them around until you can corner them in your sideburns. Lice are all over the deer when they're alive but when the carcass goes cold, as in the larder, they readily head for anything remotely warm. That must have been where I picked up mine, while moving carcasses around in the larder. Ticks have to be unplugged on a daily basis, yet the crablike lice are difficult to locate. One of the joys of deer work.

February

'Batten down the hatches' is the stern advice given by the local television weathergirl. 'There's a low coming from the west; bringing heavy rain preceded by gale-force winds.'

When I load the dogs into the truck the sky is clear, with countless twinkling stars above. A gust of wind chillier than the previous day's sweeps past me, a precursor of things to come. It comes seemingly from nowhere, catching the kennel door and slamming it hard and noisily against the frame before I can grab it. The cold blast wakes me up somewhat and is followed by another, one sharp gust following the other like waves on the sea. In contrast, overhead the stars look so calm, untouched by any of nature's wild buffeting force. They seem to stare down, unmoved, on our distant glowing planet, like the souls of once knowledgeable and superior gods.

I notice when I let the dogs out of the kennel that the increasing air movement for some unknown reason seems to excite them both. With the wind up their tails they behave more wildly, taking pleasure in chasing and snapping at the extinguished hand-sized maple leaves that parachute down from a young tree in the garden. It is going to be a day of disobedience, I can see it.

Entering the wood I check the direction of the wind, which I always do as a matter of routine. Sweeping behind me, then in an upward twist suddenly ending up in my face, it is an awkward if not impossible wind to stalk in. In the dark, with the rifle on my back, I make my way up the steep track leaning into the hill. This is my time, and I love it, free from people, just me in the woods. Closing my eyes for a short while and then opening them slowly helps to get them accustomed to the dark. I do this several times as I pass under more shadowy areas on the track but it does little to help me avoid the sticks that catch the toes of my boots, pushing the dry leaves forward. It makes an awful noise but at least the wind smothers some of the sound.

Out of the shadows the familiar shape of the big old yew tree looms, battleship grey in the darkness, just over the crest of the hill. I sit at its feet, leaning back and tucking myself into the gnarly twisted bark, at last catching my breath. I look into the sky; the clouds are colonizing it, bullying and pushing the stars away, and a steady drizzle has started. At least my natural umbrella in the form of the canopy of the great tree is keeping me dry.

The wind this morning is playing tricks, and occasionally a mini ground whirlwind sweeps low across my outstretched legs before picking up a few wet leaves and slamming them into the side of my face.

At least the light is coming now, although very slowly; I strain my eyes at something white to my right that I'm sure wasn't there when I sat down. A pair of ravens calls in the gloom, and I try unsuccessfully to pick them out through my binoculars in the poor light. I return to the white object. In bad light even common features look strange, and I can now see that what I thought was a stationary white deer is, in fact, a deer-shaped fresh chalk spill from an outlying badger hole. Incredibly, it's such a convincing deer outline that if I stare at it long enough it appears to move.

Closing my eyes I listen to the wakening birds and semi-doze for a few minutes, until the sound of a footfall on wet leaves wakes me from my slumber. The fallow doe almost steps on to me before changing its course and crossing to the other side of my huge yew. I hear her pause and stop directly behind me. The trunk separates us. What is she thinking? She can feel something isn't right but doesn't know what. For her, it is now down to pure raw instinct. Experience tells me to stay still. I can't attempt to reach for the rifle as she is too close and would sense any movement, even in the ripples that make up the wind. When her decision is made, she leaves the lee of the tree in big pronking jumps. The rifle automatically finds my shoulder and the tree holds me firm and steady as I wait in hope that the rest of the herd might follow, but none do. Although I remain under the tree until the light has wiped away all the shadows, I see no more deer in the valley or on the hillside.

The only other animal I see is a wild-eyed hare blown by the wind to the yew tree; it pauses to nip the top out of a small regen ash, its rain-drenched fur ragged in the wind. The wind forces it to move, and kicking its heels up it flashes the fluffy cream fur on the bottom of its feet.

By now the wind is becoming frantic and the rain steady. It is time to creep along the high bank, checking the valley as I go. I leave a roe buck feeding and undisturbed in the valley – bucks being currently out of season, meaning they cannot be shot – just before two chocolate-coloured shapes catch my attention: there, on the edge of a young spruce crop swaying rhythmically to and fro in the wind, are two fallow does – just what I want for this winter doe cull.

We spot each other at the same time, and like two snobbish old women they give me an uninterested glance, as though I am of no concern to them. As the cross-hairs find one of them, it turns away and fades into the background of swirling greenery, as if caught in the down draught of a helicopter. The gale has truly arrived.

My early-morning stalk is more exciting than usual today. My plan is to make it to a high seat that overlooks an opening in a large bramble-covered glade and from which there are interesting views across to the field edges. I set off early, giving myself plenty of time to get to the seat and to wait for any passing fallow. In the half-light I pick my route through a compartment of tall Douglas fir and mature larch. Many branches of various sizes have been ripped from the trees' limbs high in the tops during the night and now lie scattered about, acting as noise traps, warning every living creature that a human is in the woods. It is almost impossible to move quietly; with every step I manage to tread on a dry stick, or become ensnared in a lush branch of Douglas needles. Reaching a point when I've almost lost patience, I suddenly find myself walking at nearly normal speed and start to swagger. Then I snap another twig and have to lean against a tree, cussing, frustrated at my progress.

I'm fighting a battle with time today as daylight is keen to appear, forcing me to slow my pace in the oncoming light. I shoulder my rifle and with a slow urgency pick my route through the stick minefield. The going gets better as I reach an area of lush damp moss. It is easy to move effortlessly and silently over such ground. The light peeks through the regimented trunks of the Douglas, as rich reds and several shades of yellow emerge on the ground, rising slowly between the stark stems in shafts of colour, of life – the emergence of a new dawn.

Your senses are more acute when you're in hunting mode, and with the first rays of sun come the earthy smells of the forest: heat versus damp on the decaying fern fronds; the peaty odour of leaf-mould. And all around, unseen to all but me, a light steam rises. I move gingerly now, shooting sticks in hand, ready for a possible shot.

I glance down to avoid a moss-covered branch, and when I look up I become aware of a small object moving fast and dropping swiftly from my eye level towards my feet. What is it? My first reaction is to swipe at it with my sticks, but its speed takes me completely by surprise. I have no time to swipe, or even to move, and merely let out a frightened gasp, which sounds as stupid as I feel, as the sparrowhawk realizes its mistake and veers from my feet in a crescent-shape swoop upwards towards my face. As the bird rises we are almost eye to eye at one point. I notice that, although I am frozen solid to the ground, my breathing has quickened as though I've been running or just seen a ghost.

The whole episode lasts only seconds, but I am left in a daze and puzzled. What made it stoop at my feet? I ponder on the question for some time and come to the conclusion – maybe not the right one but good enough for me – that the bird was inexperienced, and in poor shadowy light it mistook my slow-moving feet for prey and attempted an attack. Possibly it was the low shafts of early light that confused it, for it was only in mid-swoop that the sparrowhawk realized its error. I guess, like the other mysteries in the woods, I will never really know the answer. Such is nature.

Stalking on foot this afternoon in snow, I feel the chill cutting through my clothes and sense it is going to be bitter tonight. The wind-blasted snow on the windward side of the beech trunks is already frozen solid, a sign of things to come. I open the decrepit oak wicket gate that has been here as long as I can remember, it too encased in its own veneer of ice. Freeze-dried leaves of blackthorn rattle alongside me in a stinging easterly wind. Down-trodden russet bracken hampers my every footstep.

Stopping in mid-stride I lean against the nearest tree and examine my route. As I pause, a tiny object hops across the snow and disappears in a heap of decaying branches that the sun temporarily part-thawed earlier in the day, leaving them exposed and isolated, an oasis of dark in an expanse of white. The frost has the upper hand in a landscape like this. Whatever it was I saw is small and fast, a minute black phantom, which I know instinctively is no bird.

Among the snow-splattered branches miniature cascades of dry snow fall with the movement of the unseen creature. Mounds of snow radiate away from the twig heap, creating a shallow tunnel just under the surface of the snow, similar to the sort a mole would make while worm-hunting in dry weather.

I am a lone spectator in this icy waste until suddenly a mouse explodes on to the white plain from under the surface. It is a hazardous place to be and the mouse knows it, scurrying at lightning speed across the crusty surface, then accelerating to almost a blur. A head appears from the hole in the snow where the mouse has come out – my phantom. Dressed in his winter coat, fit for any king or queen, is a stoat, pure white except for his pitch-black tail – the object that had first caught my eye. The snakelike head glances in every direction of the compass, before springing from the hole, scenting the mouse and starting the unrelenting hunt of its prey.

To see a white stoat, or ermine, in this part of the country is something quite rare. I often see them in their summer coats of russet brown and have even seen ones of mixed colour, brown and white, but the sight of that pure ermine bounding from side to side, its black tip disappearing down a hole in a sea of white, will be a memory I shall treasure.

It's amazing what you see if you make the effort to get up early and go out into the woods.

This morning, while I'm dragging a fallow buck fawn to the truck, a fox crosses my path carrying a massive black rabbit. Such an oversized prize reminds me of when I once saw a petite vixen carrying a huge cock pheasant in its mouth. The fox looked so small and the bird so large that the vixen's struggle to manoeuvre her prey over an assault course of restricting woodland debris looked oddly comical. I managed to get so close to her that I could hear her sniffing and snuffling, blowing air through her nose in an attempt to clear the mass of feathers that was obstructing her limited vision. The resolve of this animal in her uphill challenge was unrelenting and an inspiration to me.

Animals, although often referred to as dumb, are, when fully appreciated, far from it. I believe that they act and behave on a different plane to us humans, and have evolved ways of coping with problems in life that should be admired and, in many cases, mirrored by us.

Fallow do not appear tonight, though when I leave the wood my headlights pick out a group moving to and from the neighbour's ground. I will have to admit defeat and see if the forester will temporarily fence. The pattern of behaviour has changed, the deer becoming increasingly nocturnal and leaving the area well before light to return to the safety of the neighbouring land.

I finally reach the high seat in the dark. The weather looks unpromising, and sudden gusts rock the seat as though it's a ship on the sea, swirling me around in circles. Above me black clouds pass, making smokers' rings across the face of the moon. Occasionally a shaft of light crests the rim of a cloud, emerging into the dark like angel's wings. Undaunted, the moon looks down as the maelstrom of cloud gathers and ripples, only to tumble, briefly swiping at her face before being driven on by an uncontrollable wind. Throughout, her dignity is ever-present; unmovable she remains shrouded in a halo of brightness and light.

At my level, on the seat, the weather is no less unforgiving; sudden gusts grab the pole-sized spruce that I am attached to, sending the top into a pirouetting spiral. Glassing the ground from my twisting eyrie, I can pick out nothing moving in the gloom around me. Half closing my eyes and leaning back into the seat, I think back to the warmth of my bed; daylight is a long time coming today. I can only endure the wait, shrug from within and shiver. I pull the rifle in closer to my groin, as if it could lend me warmth.

With nothing happening on the ground I soon lose interest, my eyes instinctively searching the forest roof above me instead. Under a partially dawning sky the squirrels are already active high in the tops of the beech trees, seeking out the large buds, scouring the canopy, traversing silhouettes in a world of tempest and wind-hurled leaves.

Slowly the dark releases its hold, black turning un-noticed to grey – fallow time!

My activity in the seat has attracted the attention of one of my nocturnal neighbours. As I glance once more to ground level, a small mixed group of fallow approach from behind. Standing stock-still and alert, the lead doe scans me. I dare not move. The sound of waking birds becomes enhanced. My body is a coiled spring. My mind races through several scenarios, some reminding me of the consequences of making a stupid, rushed decision, such as the one where the doe leads the herd in a sudden dash as I move towards my rifle; or the one where they walk off, backsides facing me, so that I am unable to take the shot no matter how close they are to me. But my favourite, and the one that plays out, is the timed decision to allow her to lose interest in me, and then, as the herd moves away past the seat, to slowly pull the rifle to my shoulder, select a victim, call out, 'Morning!' to stop them, and then carefully squeeze the trigger.

By the time I drag my cull up to the truck, the early-morning start is already forgotten.

Births and deaths go on all the time in the forest, mostly unseen. When you witness one such event it leaves you feeling not only lucky but also privileged to have seen it. Though being in the woods can be frustrating, it's never boring as there's always something of interest to watch, observe and learn from.

This morning holds one such event for me. I am sitting in the high seat in the larch trees, void now of most of their russet-yellow tinged needles. In front of the seat is a small open area of bramble and snow-swept bracken. When time allows I like to get this area cut on a yearly cycle to help with deer control and also to save the ground flora from scrub invasion.

After glassing around the glade for what seems like the hundredth time, my attention is taken by the large numbers of woodpigeon that have alighted around the seat, high above me in the stark, bare branches. The wind sways these plump, dumpy birds up and down until a nervous neighbour, for whatever reason, panics the rest into flight with an enormous amount of wing noise. Several of the birds return after climbing high into the sky and making one or two whip cracks with their wings in a form of display. One bird lands just behind a trunk of larch so that I am shielded from its vision. I take a closer look at it.

Pigeons, like several common British birds, are easily overlooked almost to the point of being taken for granted. From a distance they appear grey, like nothing special, but close up they abound with colour – sheens of blue, green and white flecks, and chests of salmon pink.

I am wrapped up in the pigeons when a squeak below

the seat catches my attention. I look down to see a mouse scrabble at lightning speed across a dead branch that had been felled and left to rot, followed by another, then another, all clambering over the entanglement of dead branches. More and more mice leave the woodpile, diving off and disappearing into the dense undergrowth. Something is approaching, alarming them; it must be close now as mice are throwing themselves off the structure of sticks and plummeting to the ground.

The scene reminds me of an African plain in miniature, filled with panicking wildebeest and zebra, the predatory lion soon appearing in the shape of a tiny weasel. The pocket-sized lion is not to be sidetracked and pursues the smell of the mice, moving so fast that it appears to skim over the branches like a tanned hovercraft, hoovering up the scent. I watch in envy at its endless energy as it plunges again to the ground, then reappears on the branches just as quickly. On its third descent into the maze of sticks, I hear, but can't see, a skirmish taking place below a commotion of sharp shrill squeaks. It does not seem possible that the weasel can have got back on to the sticks without me noticing it, but it is no apparition that sits triumphant on the stick pile with a mouse dangling from its mouth.

We humans have a saying when we lose a loved one: life goes on. And sure enough, just like us, as I sit perched in my seat up high like a god looking down on his subjects, one by one, over the course of the morning, the inhabitants of the woodpile return to their stick kingdom to carry on with the struggle that is life.

The nocturnal phone call wakes me with a start and leaves me with a headache for the rest of the day. I must sound pretty stupid on the phone as I was well into a deep sleep when it rang.

I listen as best as I can, assuring the caller with a grunt that I am the stalker for that area. The police woman on the other end sounds as though she's in a hurry, rushing through the limited information that she passes on to me, everything said in such haste that I'm unable to absorb it fully. Well before I can question her she is gone, and I am left holding the receiver in the dark wondering why I ever offered to help with road-traffic accidents involving deer.

It's strange, but the more I try to get up quietly without waking the rest of the household, the worse it is; the locks on the gun cabinet open almost mischievously, with a rebellious attitude, breaking the silence with a metallic clunk. Drunk with sleep, I stagger in the dark, catching my clothes on well-known door handles as I blunder around the house looking for the equipment that I will need.

The cold outside soon wakes me up, and the ice on the road keeps me alert. The information was vague; I like as much detail as possible when I get called to an

RTA. The police car is at the scene, its blue lights flashing, and I breathe a sigh of relief as I approach it. First, I have found the right place, and second, it's easier to do the job with an extra pair of hands. Folks who have been involved in an accident and have hit a deer can turn on you sometimes if you have to put it out of its misery, so it's always reassuring to have an officer on the scene. As I pull up behind the police car, though, I am flabbergasted when it lets out its siren as a sign of recognition and then drives off. With the bright flashing light gone, I am once more plunged into the world of dark alone.

So here I am at 2.30 a.m., in the frost, looking for a deer that could be injured or dying in the blackness. At least the road is quiet. Scanning the road edges my spotlight doesn't find any pairs of eyes, just the glint of glass from a beer bottle some idiot has thrown out of their car while on the move. It landed well within the hedge, and has me fooled for a while.

My dog is excited about being in harness and starts leaping like a husky when I attach his fluorescent collar with the hawkbell. Even this early, occasional lights of cars come past us and slow, their occupants wondering what we are doing. My dog and I wander the length of the road until he finally takes some real interest; with the light of the torch I see the flash of coloured glass from the car that struck the deer.

Things start to look up as the trail gets easier, and our

pace quickens. Once under the barbed wire I am on a
farmer's land that I have permission to shoot on. Then
the dog leaps high again near a hedge and I know we are
close. Although the dog is keen to go, I sit him on the
spot and use the torch to scan the inside of the hedge. A
pair of soulful eyes meet mine. Eyes can tell you a lot,
and these are lost eyes, like those of a dog that has been
beaten, unable, no matter what it does, to please its
master. This deer has given up on life. I feel for the poor
fallow buck, lying injured in the hedge, and end his pain
without any qualms, for no wild animal with a will to
live would let you get as close as I manage to in order
to dispatch him without a struggle.

This late into the season it's a waste of time and effort
even attempting to stalk fallow does on foot. I'm sure
they have eyes that can see through trees and hearing that
can detect me even as I leave my house.

Fallow stalking becomes a matter of ambushing, sometimes called bush-whacking, which involves waiting
undetected as the deer go about their business within the
forest. Trying to outsmart the deer can be a chore on its
own, and with reduced numbers in a big block of woodland the chances of them passing your position are fairly
limited. You have to attempt to be in the right place at
the right time as they pass.

This morning is no different to usual. I placed the high seat in position in the dark the previous night. Now, at first light, the sky is full of strange-shaped crimson clouds that appear to hang from the heavens like upside-down mountains. The image is endless, an infinite pattern of landscape views. I sit in my seat watching as the clouds jostle positions, ever changing, within minutes taking the shape of Antarctic ice pressure ridges erupting through encrusted snow. Above this scene, narrow horizontal streaks of orange and gold attempt to peep and flicker around the ridge of grey cloud resembling an ancient galleon.

I turn my attention to the landscape around me. Through a fir screen of bottle green a lone silver birch stem shines out, thrusting itself into my vision with a seemingly special need to be noticed. The dogwood bushes look spectacular with their blood-red leaves, old berries hanging like jewellery from the plant. Draped around the shoulders of the dogwood, like a cloak of royal ermine, the fluffy seed heads of old man's beard thread themselves between its branches. When the breeze finally parts the low, ground-hugging mists, I get a chance to glimpse the steep grassy slopes opposite and beyond through the yellowing peppered leaves of the birch.

I listen to the bird calls, naming each species in my mind: the rasping jay; a long note from a distant nuthatch; and, closer, the pip-pip of the robin, all entwined with the laughing tones of the green woodpecker. A lone raven croaks, its call growing louder and then fading, while above me a territorial buzzard cries its disgust at the raven, at what it sees as misuse of its airspace.

Behind me in the Christmas-tree plantation, dozens upon dozens of silhouetted pigeons noisily leave their overnight roost site, heading for their day-feeding grounds like bees exiting a hive. Then, not quite believing what I am seeing, I spot a small group of fallow, walking in a direction I never thought they would, in the same ride that I used to approach the seat. They must be able to smell my scent on the grass, still shrouded in ground mist, but they seem oblivious to it. They take me by surprise, making their entrance like this, but I still manage to drop one.

March

At last it is the end of the winter doe cull, which gives me a part break from the early starts and late-night finishes. It's a joy in itself not to have to unlock the rifle safe. While starting work slightly later today, I can't help myself and already in my mind I start arranging and organizing all the jobs, other than shooting, that will need doing this coming season.

I must visit the gunsmith for the yearly service check and maintenance. Before putting the weapons in the truck, I double-check that all the guns are unloaded, and do the same checks again at the dealer's. It's a form of routine, almost a ritual, that I go through; you can never be too safe.

It's a real day of grey today, the empty sky blending into the colourless earth with no divide, like an endless veil. On this windless day, a lone pigeon-sized bird of prey courses low over the fields, gliding and twisting in a slow determined flight. As it turns and heads towards my stationary truck, the wings appear to form a V. The black on the ends of the wing-tips makes it look as though the bird has dipped its primaries in a pot of dark paint. I identify the bird as a visiting male hen harrier. I am surprised how thorough his hunting technique is, covering the ground in sharp sweeps and turns, yet looking completely relaxed in flight. As he rises and twists over the vehicle I notice that, like a barn owl, he makes no noise as he cuts overhead through the still, moist air.

First red admiral today. This fast-flying, rich blood-red-coloured insect flies inside the cab of the truck. I'm unsure whether any overwinter here. Possibly they hibernate in sheds or in other weatherproof shelters. Or perhaps it's the first migrant to reach our shores? Like most, if not all, butterflies, its life is linked to certain species of plant, and in the case of the red admiral it's the stinging nettle on which it lays its eggs.

On the side of a ride, on a carpet of discarded dry Corsican pine needles, I find the remains of a partially skinned carcass of a male adder, killed and eaten by a buzzard. In the past I have watched adders and smooth snakes taken by birds of prey and corvids, but what makes this find more interesting is that, only last year, the same incident happened to another male adder, almost to the day, in almost – literally within feet of – the same spot in the forest.

Many times I have observed different species of birds of prey favouring certain trees and branches when hunting, in particular those that give both clear vision and access to the forest floor. A favourite trick of the sparrowhawk and buzzard is to use a series of wind-bent branches on the ride edge to fly on to and observe from. Then, if nothing of interest is seen, they slowly and silently flight their way up the ride to the next windblown perch.

Today I see my first pale yellow brimstone butterfly; it is the colour, flitting about on the newly cut growth of a winter coppice area, that first catches my eye. The brimstone male is an eye-catching yellow and the female a lighter shade, almost white. The sight of this insect in the forest is a sure sign of spring and a promise that better weather is on its way, though not necessarily imminent. Of all butterflies, I think it appears the most delicate, as looks as though it's made of crêpe paper.

Now the weather has warmed a little, it's time to set up my squirrel trap line. Squirrels do enormous amounts of damage to many species of trees within the forest. Grey squirrels are non-native to our country, unlike our smaller red squirrel. The poor reds are not as competitive as the larger, stronger greys, which have increased in numbers, pushing the reds up to our most northern borders.

However, it's not all doom and gloom; greys can benefit the woods by killing a small number of trees, as all forests benefit from a percentage of dead wood. Dead trees left standing are food and home for insects, and the insects are then fed on by wild birds. Dead wood is also home to many species of birds and mammals. Fungus and beetles then make use of the fallen giants brought down in a storm, forming an ecosystem of their own. But too many squirrels can leave the forest short of future healthy trees, so the number of grey squirrels does have to be regulated.

Twice a day I check the cage traps in which the captives are caught alive. Trapping only reduces numbers and certainly does not exterminate them, which wouldn't, in any case, be feasible. Trapping is only one tool of the suite used to control them. Like deer, grey squirrels have no real native predators to prey on them, and left unchecked their numbers can spiral out of control; and any great increase can be detrimental to the forest environment.

There is a big difference for me between stalking as a job and recreational stalking at the weekend. It's easy to get too concerned with numbers and put yourself under mental pressure when working alone. Trying to keep the majority of farmers and most foresters happy is almost an impossible task, for the number of deer they would truly like to see is zero. Recreational stalking in my own time is somewhat different, as I go when I want to go, not when I feel I should go.

My private piece of ground gives me enough joy through my just being there, let alone shooting there. The area itself is a mixture of field systems, sometimes flooded, and small woods and copses that reach down to the sea and salt marshes. On the fringes is another set of separate, stand-alone habitats of both wet and dry lands, the heath home to many rare reptiles and amphibians. It is heaven on earth.

Tall reeds hide a large herd of resident sika deer for a good part of the year, but at certain times in the seasons you can witness the amazing sight of these wonderful deer, who have always been my favourites. On still summer evenings I watch them beachcombing in and around the sandy tussocks, while in the autumn I delight in the primeval fury of the rut, the fights and the shrieks of stags throughout the nights. In winter, the weather can change this region into a wild place, as wild at times as the Arctic, or so it seems to me. Huge delinquent sleet squalls can level swathes of the reed beds, flooding the black sunken-mud ditches in a relentless fury of ice, water and wind. To be out on a night like that ignites your imagination.

On a balmy summer's night, though, it is hard to remember the wind, the biting sleet harassing frozen cheeks, the torchlight that struggles with the dark streaks of ice when you're out collecting the evening's harvest of carcasses as spectral harbour buoys flash in the distance. It's cold, it's wet and it can be scary.

The deer leave their daytime resting places at almost last light. I have positioned a high seat in an old oak on the edge of the field where it joins the marsh that overlooks open water in the bay.

On the marsh, if you strain your ears, the calls of the oystercatcher and curlew are picked up on the air and blown across the writhing reed tops. Small flocks of black duck skim the waves, overhead geese call out their rhythmic cascades of tales of wild places. I listen as the clamour dies away and the birds disappear into the blackness of thunderhead-shaped clouds.

The richness of my stalking area cannot be measured: to be silent and alone in such a place, to witness the sights and sounds, whatever the season, leaves you richer, so who cares if you don't shoot anything?

My first thought is that it's a solitary sika stag way out on the marsh, and to put distance between it and myself I actually crawl to the safety of the sea wall, where I can finally stand upright and stretch my back. Content that I have not been seen, I am in no hurry and merely stroll with the wind in my face to the ridge of the rush-covered bank. Spreading myself low I level my binoculars at the dark object within the reeds. Eventually, after what seems like a long time, the wind parts the reeds enough for a good view. It is no sika stag that I see, unless it is able to sit on the wreckage of an old fence stake.

From my viewpoint the bird appears huge, my binoculars exaggerating its size. My first marsh harrier. The gold crown tells me it is a female; she looks a heavyweight in the bird world. The number of times I have flicked through the pages of my guide book and admired this bird, and now here she is. With no deer to be seen, I preoccupy myself with my newfound friend, who sits motionless, unconcerned by me or anything else. Not even the attentions of a crow trouble her.

After an hour the harrier shakes herself, fluffing up her feathers, which make her look the size of an eagle. I half expect her to call out in a regal voice to tell the bird kingdom that the queen of the marsh is in the air when she finally leaves her post. Instead, like an assassin, she slips low, coursing in between the reed glades.

Flocks of waders leave the estuary, erupting skywards, twisting away from the dark harrier shape in a panicking mass. Larger waders push their bodies into the mud, hoping not to be noticed. Several times I watch the harrier pounce on something on the edges of the reeds, but it is too far for me to see what has fallen victim. After her eighth pounce I notice a small dark object clutched in her clasped talons. There is no jubilant cry; the call instead is high, soft and long, unlike a hawk. As she skims over the drying straw-coloured reeds I lose sight of her behind a thin veil of low clouds.

For me, another sign of spring is the sight of your first adder. The soul feels that the weather's warming up and so your senses heighten, and the adders must feel the same.

The first to emerge are the males, short and thick in body, fresh out of hibernation. Contrary to popular belief, adders are not short-tempered, and you can approach them at this time of year quite closely. The males enjoy lying out on a sunny spring morning, basking on the dry pine needles caught within the lower branches of a pine in a cascade, but now cast from the tree. Once on the floor the needles extract and retain that extra warmth from the weak March sun.

Many forest walkers have a fear of the adder, and if you get up close enough you can see the copper-red eyes that make him look angry. As with most wildlife, it is more scared of you than you are of it. As the saying goes – and it's sound advice – you leave them alone and they will leave you alone. Having toiled in the forest almost every working day, I have never felt threatened or had a bad experience with the adder; in fact, it's the reverse. I actually look forward to my first meeting with this sentry to the gates of spring.

We humans seem to spend much of our time making judgements about who is good-looking and who, like me, never went to handsome school. Beauty, it is said, is only skin deep, and some religions teach that the body is a mere shell, that even the most hideous-looking person has something to bring to the table of life. I do hope so. It is the same in the world of nature – things are not always what they seem. How can you compare, for example, the brilliant colours of the ordinary-sounding bullfinch to the drab appearance of the wren, whose wonderful, melodic song is almost hypnotic?

There is one bird I look forward to hearing more than any other at this time of year. When you first hear her calling out her own name it is usually from the tip of a freshly foliated lime-green birch. So sweet are the initial irregular calls that I am forced to listen and linger: 'Chiff chaff, chiff chaff, chiff chaff.'

April

Today I notice a dark tan butterfly, its ragged, torn outline giving its species away. It whisks past me, sailing on the stiff breeze, its agile, flowing flight resembling that of an oak leaf blown along on the wind. I follow its progress until it comes to rest on a sunlit field maple leaf on the corner of the ride; it is almost impossible to see. The comma butterfly, with its amazing disappearing camouflage, rests on the damp leaf and is instantly shrivelled, absorbed into the field craft of nature.

Spring is a good time to spot stoats and weasels, for at this time of year they are hunting for food for their young. In the wilds you come across them more by chance than skill: a glimpse of a quick-moving small animal streaking in almost a blur across the road; or a short, chance meeting on a forest track.

Both the stoat and its smaller cousin, the weasel, are elusive, keeping well out of the way of man, and for good reason. Gamekeepers persecute them, even today, by setting tunnel traps, knowing well that the species

Mustelidea are extremely curious about investigating holes and tunnels. Many have perished that way. With modern game-rearing techniques I'm not fully convinced of the argument for killing them. In fact, I would imagine the car is a bigger killer of young pheasant poults than an army of stoats or weasels.

Today, a pair of stoats crosses the road in front of the truck and, personally, I am glad to see them: natural, ancient little helpers controlling rabbit populations like they have always done, mostly out of sight of man.

Without even looking to the sky, I hear a sound and recognize a friendly chatter from the air.

Long missed, but never forgotten, like the call of the first visiting fieldfare, one a song of summer, the other of winter, and equal in my appreciation. A welcome voice and always a joy to hear, a natural calendar within my life, a reminder of things to do, of things left undone, a prompt: the trill chittering of our own bluebird, the swallow.

With sickle wings and extensive tail, swallows slice through the warm spring air. My first pair of the season is freshly returned from as far away as Africa. Once their territories have been established the swallows will become a common sight, flying low over the stock fields, their happy voices taken for granted amid the chorus of summer.

I have a great view of a low-flying kingfisher as it passes me, not even slowing down on the bend in the stream, a bird always in a hurry. Even when it streaks under a large willow that casts dappled shade on to the bank and water, the tree's shadow does nothing to dull the brilliance of this bird's incredible fluorescent metallic colours. With its tropical look, this is a truly beautiful bird of orange and hot-summer-sky blue, striking in colour and flight, a miniature Concorde of the bird world.

Deer creep about in all manner of places, both day and night. Somehow, judging by the fraying on the recently planted spruce, at least two roe bucks have taken up residence between the main road and an army petroleum depot. Both bucks must have used the residential gardens and hedges as access to secure a territory within the so-called fenced area. It's certainly going to be both time-consuming and challenging to catch up with them. At least they are roe deer, which are more predictable than the herding species.

When I worked on a private country estate, I had two older colleagues, both of whom had fought in the Second World War. One had fought Germans, the other had pursued the Japanese. They would argue about the nations they had fought, each giving examples of why their enemy was the worst. Many hours were spent on wet days in old wooden sheds within the woods, or at times under a hurriedly put-up piece of tarpaulin, debating the subject.

It can be a bit like this in the deer world, with each stalker claiming his or her species is harder to cull than a neighbour's. I've found herding deer more difficult: sika deer get smart very quickly and wild fallow can rapidly become wise and cunning. Both species under pressure soon learn the value of becoming nocturnal and avoiding strategically placed permanent high seats. The fallow on my beat can at times be very stupid and let their guard down, but most of the time they are as wild as the wind itself.

Fallow always seem as though they are in a hurry to get somewhere, constantly on the move, unless resting under some impenetrable cover. Stalking them on foot in the winter is next to impossible. With pheasant shoots and hunting going on all around you, stalking on foot makes as much sense as stalking an SAS trooper while dressed in a bright, noisy clown suit.

At times, it seems that the only place you will see fallow still and quiet, presenting themselves for an easy shot, is on a skyline – or perhaps, like the roe buck I have just spotted, who is practically grinning at me, standing alongside a large petroleum tank, its red-letter sign reading: WARNING: DO NOT PUNCTURE.

Shot three young roe bucks this morning, none of them over three years. For me, down south, it pays to cull bucks early in the season before the summer growth comes up and provides hiding places for them.

I'm happy to see my first orange-tip butterfly of this season. The orange on the wing-tips of the male makes this unmistakable butterfly visible from a great distance and one of the easiest to spot. I normally see my first one on the road edges in spring, seeking out the mustard plants where they lay their eggs.

My birthday. It's funny, but I've never liked shooting anything on my birthday. I'll carry on with the cull tomorrow; one day should not make that much difference. Instead I will check all the restock sites (recently planted areas) for the presence of pine weevil. These little demons bite huge chunks of bark from the newly planted pine and if left undiscovered can cause massive damage to the plantation, similar to that inflicted by squirrels on hardwoods. Criss-crossing the site I look for fresh exposed weeping bite marks, the telling signs. Individual trees are searched at ground level because the beetles have a self-protective habit of falling or jumping off the tree when you touch it. These sites need constant visits and records kept as an infestation can soon occur. Luckily, today I find none.

Back to the cull. I manage to get two spike roe bucks this morning. Being young and not wood-wise yet, they can be reasonably easy to shoot, more naive about stalking mistakes than a doe or older buck. That is, as long as you remain downwind of them. Later in the day's stalking, through a patchy morning mist, I come across a middle-aged roe buck fraying some young Douglas fir trees on the edge of a two-year plant site.

The first temptation on coming across such a scene is to shoot the offender, believing that will solve the problem. You may solve it temporarily, but more deer will take the last one's place and each buck will fray more trees to show ownership; the more bucks the more damage, so I don't feel guilty about sparing this one! Bearing in mind also that roe are territorial, and the buck was in good health, I decide to leave him as a security buck, his job to patrol, my ears and eyes on the site when I'm not around, ready to push any younger bucks away.

Fresh fraying always looks worse than it actually is, and there is natural regeneration to replace deer-damaged trees.

Today I have a German client with me who's come for a few days' stalking. He is no problem on the range regarding accuracy; it's his gun handling that leaves room for improvement. He is certainly not up to my standard.

After a little episode in the woods I have to rein him in. In Germany, and elsewhere on the Continent it seems, there are numerous traditions involved in stalking and hunting. One of them is new to me. Basically, if you are older than the resident stalker or guide, apparently you, *the visitor*, know the ground better than your guide within a day. I'm also informed that deer don't come out in the rain, and other such nonsense.

It amazes me how some people manage to get older without getting any wiser. Everything I have learnt has been given to me by the forest, and if the lesson is a good working practice I use it. This client wants to stop in areas where I never see deer and gets restless in areas where I want deer shot. Strange.

German man sulking.

The next day. German man still sulking.

Today I am a god. The client even attempts to kiss me. Until I tell him to push off, that is, and explain what will happen if he ever tries that again. But it doesn't seem to curb his admiration for me. He can't praise me enough. And this is all down to a trophy roe buck which I first spotted last year, but only twice, and who returned today to our stalking ground.

It lived in the forest but also spent time in its territory, which covered the neighbour's ground, a wildlife trust reserve. Although I can admire a trophy buck, I must admit I struggle with the idea of trophy shooting, even though I have shot such deer in my career. At work I find more satisfaction in having a reason to dispatch an injured or sick animal. And this buck was old. In fact, I was always astonished at the distance he covered considering his age.

This morning I find him patrolling in the damp early mist. We are both walking, and then we spot each other simultaneously. He stares at me, I at him, both surprised – him to see anyone and me to see him. Under my breath, I request the client to shoot him. He obliges and the buck falls: a medal buck. This is when the attempted kiss takes place. For the next twenty minutes, my ears hurt with the bragging of what a great hunter he is. It seems to slip his mind that the poor old buck was standing only twenty metres from him. I almost say, but hold back, that shooting a medal buck is no different from shooting a doe, and it certainly does not make you a better stalker.

There is an old country saying which claims that whatever you are doing when you hear your first cuckoo you will be doing for the rest of the year. I hope it's not true as all these early mornings are taking their toll.

His arrival is late this year; I glimpse the grey hawk bird as he flies across an open area of recently planted Scots pine. The male bird calls out 'Cuckoo!' several times and then alights on a tall pine tree it has singled out. I think of the journey this bird has made from Africa and marvel at the cuckoo's stamina. The male arrives first, with the females following a few weeks later. I've seen several in the air at once, males and females, some birds making strange babbling, bubbling sounds.

It's always good to hear your first cuckoo, but sitting in a high seat for several hours listening to the constant clamour of a group of them can drive you nuts. And although I love the cries of the buzzards soaring high on the thermals, the continual calling from chick to parent can also fray your nerves.

Today I have one of those unreal experiences that make you pinch yourself to check you're awake because you can't believe what you're seeing.

I am with another stalking client, and we are walking with our rifles on our shoulders, the guest shadowing my every step. It is hardly light, the morning fog like a haze hugging the ground. I have to work hard, straining to see. I keep my eyes forward, yet know in my mind it is still too dark to shoot even if we see something shootable.

As I walk the ride my eyes water and I have to stop and wipe them slowly on the sleeve of my coat. As I search the gloom again, I pick up a black dot, small and fast, racing towards us along a tractor rut. I raise my hand and hear the client stop in mid-stride: he asks in a hushed, dry voice, 'What do you see?' The object is still hurtling towards us, too close for me to answer. Out of the smoky ground haze a hare appears, eyes bulging, ears pressed flat to its head. It passes us, brushing our boots without even slowing.

I have no time to turn around to the client, who lets out a giggle of delight, as my vision is now locked on to something larger, also travelling fast in the same direction as the hare and down the very same rut. It, too, has its ears pressed tight to its head, resembling a greyhound.

The vixen notices me only seconds before she is about to plough into my legs. I feel my body brace, expecting the impact, and find myself unintentionally twisting my body sideways to the fox. Instead of hitting me, she leaps, sidestepping me to my right. At only an arm's length and at shoulder height, the look on the vixen's face says it all. In mid-flight her legs move in slow, running motions, like a racehorse clearing a tall jump, and that's when our eyes met. Under her exposed belly the udder sweeps from side to side. Like an arched bullet, she hits the ground running, disappearing as fast as she arrived.

This time I do look back at my guest. We both grin at

first, and then burst out laughing, forgetting where we are and the fact we're supposed to be stalking in silence.

It is a truly great day and an unforgettable experience for both of us.

Today I see a good number of my first chocolate butterflies high in the air. Not so dissimilar to other dark species that frequent the woodlands, the speckled wood is found early in the season. They seem later this year – I usually see them in March.

What I like about this butterfly is that it is an adaptable species, travelling everywhere in the woods. You see them high in the canopy or holding aerial dogfights, spiralling after one another in a shaft of sunlight, struggling between the trees, or simply basking, wings outstretched on a sunlit bramble leaf. When it is really warm and the puddles in the forest dry up, you see dozens crowding around a small patch of mud, extracting what moisture they can.

Unlike other sun-loving butterflies, the speckled wood will tolerate the shadier parts of the forest. At a distance it looks fairly plain, but close up it has intricate yellowish spots and darker patterns on its wings. Like most of its brethren it possesses the ability to melt into the shrubbery. Once perched on a tall grass stem, its wings shut, it can remain entirely hidden, soaking up the spring sun.

I arrive in the forest late in the afternoon and the dogs are keen to get out of the vehicle after being shut up for most of the day. Unusually for them, as soon as the door is partially opened, they both spill out. Like me they are glad to be back in the wood. On our patrols it's easy to slip into the habit of taking the same old tried and tested routes; I suppose I tend to do this without even thinking. But today I decide to change my routine and take an unfamiliar track through some mature Douglas fir.

The forest floor under the high dense canopy is almost bare except for a few large limbs that have been snapped and torn off in high winds and tossed to the ground. Three quarters of the way through the plantation, both dogs pause. When they stop, I stop – I've learnt to trust them – and study the direction of their stares, but I see nothing. It is easy walking, and quiet too: in fact, on the carpet of moss we are now walking on you can tread as quietly as a household cat.

At the edge of the plantation is the fence line that I want to check. The fence check is uneventful; no holes are found. Then, on the way back, both dogs pause again. Although we are not following a track, I recognize certain damaged limbs on the trees and realize that we are back at the very same spot where the dogs hesitated earlier.

Sitting both dogs down, I walk forward. I've taken only a few steps when a scream makes me almost leap on to the nearest low-flying cloud. Perhaps it's the effect of the shadowy surroundings, or the vibration of the scream, but to me it sounds like a baby being slaughtered; either way, I know this sound, but it does not immediately register or stop my heart from missing a beat. The creature screams out again, just as terribly as the first time, but this time I am ready, and the pitiful cry finds its way into my very core. Again and again it screams. I have heard this cry before; it has been catalogued and stored, but never has it sounded so awful. I still can't see where the noise is coming from, but I know it is being made by a hare.

Turning to the dogs I follow their fixed stares: when pitted against their senses, you soon realize how crude ours are. The screaming continues and I search with my binoculars the heap of brash it seems to be coming from. It is only a mix of several branches and yellowing, decaying needles, but still I can't see anything. Fiddling with my binoculars I suddenly focus on two small faces that peer out from between a patch of russet-coloured foliage. I stand like a statue and the pair of stoats soon lose interest. On this natural stage I can now see the whole scene unfolding.

The pair have pinned down a terrified young leveret. The normally creamy-white chests of the stoats' bibs are the colour of a slaughter-man's apron. I am torn with guilt, and wonder whether I should intervene, although I know that would be the wrong move. Luckily for me the screams weaken, so my decision is made for me: better to let nature take its course. I watch as, one at a time, the stoats attempt to silence the leveret. As one of them drags the corpse away to another small heap of denser brash, I check my watch. It has taken the stoats four minutes to kill the hare – hardly the one bite to the neck of the prey that is so widely reported.

Back at the truck I praise the dogs for doing so well with all the action and noise, and, in the very last moments of dusk, I ponder on the role that I play in the deer's lives as their predator. Did those four minutes, I ask myself, feel like a lifetime to the poor leveret? My unseen bullet, according to the ballistics on the box, travels at 2,939 feet per second to get the same result. But how can I think ill of the stoats' techniques? After all, they are driven by a need for survival.

There is a strange fact of life I can never fathom, and that is how man struggles to live alongside animal competition. Many times in my life I have had to listen to keepers who have lost the odd pheasant to a fox almost spitting blood out of pure hate for the fox. Once they have calmed down, with the next breath they will cheerfully demonstrate how on a beaters' shoot they managed to knock down a dozen pheasants on just one drive!

They are surely missing a point here. Sport is separate from survival. We kill for fun; animals kill on instinct. Large numbers of birds killed in a pen by any predator are not killed for fun or because the predator is evil, as I've heard it said. Evil is man-made; the fox kills instinctively, caching away what he can for when times are hard, whether we like it or not.

Understanding nature is what makes being in the woods so interesting. You see the everyday struggles that most people miss out on. Over many years this working insight gives you clues as to what's happening or what might be about to happen unseen in the foliage around you and in the canopy above. Generally, people stroll around oblivious to signs, scents and smells, not seeing or hearing the information that is provided like the pages of an unfolding story.

Jays have many different calls, and certain individuals give voice with personalized tones. Some have rasping cries; others sound similar to the European nutcracker, loud and coarse; some have almost parrotlike qualities. Jays are like mynah birds – they are exceptionally superb mimics, copying not only their fellow woodland birds and indeed other jays that they have heard, but also birds they have come across on their travels.

The call of a curlew draws my attention today as I am going round my squirrel hoppers. There is no water for several miles and I have never heard one in the vicinity before. So, in such an unusual setting for curlew, I listen for it to call out again. It does, and I can tell it's calling from somewhere high up in the top of an old oak tree.

Shielding my eyes from the streaming, flickering sun, I struggle to view anything in the dense, shadowy branches. Strange indeed. I trace the sound to an area tight to the main trunk of the oak. Luckily, today the breeze is stronger and higher in the tree and a sudden sharp gust helps uncover the source: a very anxious-looking jay. Its body language indicates it is fearful, nervous; it obviously knows I am here and would normally have flown off, but something, hidden from me, is keeping it there.

Jays prefer to avoid contact with man, always fluttering a safe distance away, but this one remains glued to the branch in fright. I search the direction in which the bird is looking but the lush greenery reveals nothing. Then, giving the call of a blackbird, the jay hurls itself into flight, alighting abruptly on a lower branch, closer to me, and only now do I see the problem: perched on a branch, slightly higher than the jay, is a very large, fierce-looking female sparrowhawk. Little wonder the jay was terrified. The sparrowhawk ignores me; her bright, piercing yellow eyes burrow into the jay, her full concentration on the hunt. In desperation the jay kwicks like a wood owl, several times, to upset the hawk, playing out a role that must have succeeded in the past. But the hunter will not be intimidated – its gaze never leaves the jay.

Aware of its impending doom the poor jay fluffs its feathers, forlorn and lost; it has tried every trick it knows. The life-and-death decision is then made: the jay loses its nerve and gives flight. Behind it, gaining, the dark shape of the hunter looms, the hen sparrowhawk body being well adapted for flying low between the extensive branches. The jay's fate was sealed the moment it left the comparative safety of the screen of leaves. Flying away and low, it screams out all its fear to the world over the top of a hazel thicket. I watch nature take its course as a puff of feathers tumbles to the earth from the sky.

The long shadow of my truck races the double roadside hedge, which is bathed in a cheerful orange glow. The shadow flows smoothly through and over it, sprinting across the top and caressing the sides.

It is the last hour of evening sun, a beautiful night and unusually warm. Newly hatched micro midges, brought out by the day's heat, dance in their thousands. Swarming in natural chandeliers, they hover over the road ahead, before sacrificing themselves on to the windscreen.

I am in a hurry to check a handful of squirrel traps in an outlying block before night falls. Abandoning the vehicle at the barrier, I pause on a steep incline to catch my breath. It's quite pleasing to see the dogs doing the same.

The ravens that I know in this area slink away from their nest; as they are secretive birds I have only to enter the wood to make them jumpy. Slipping from its nest a female takes a low erupting flight followed by some minimal slow wing-beats to make her retreat.

Even from my halfway vantage point I have long-distance farmland and countryside views rolling away from me. Bright yellow fields of rape, hedges and small sheep fields, all glazed in an evening light of crimson and gold that washes around me on a cooling breeze.

At the top of the hill, and before I even get to the trap, I know I have a catch, for the sound of two angry male squirrels greets me, scolding each other and me as I approach.

The type of trap I use catches them live, and I visit all the traps at least twice a day. This evening produces several squirrels that are quickly and quietly dispatched; if these animals are left to their own devices they can soon ravage the tops of the trees within this high-quality stand of beech.

So foxes *can* live with badgers in the same sett. Tonight I see one leave and cross the track in front of me, its fur coated in the same fine sandstone as that of the badgers who live there and who I have watched so many times.

May

A badger-watching evening. I check the wind and decide to wait on the trunk of an old oak that has been wind-blown for years. Some reasonably heavy rain squalls have made the forest floor damp and uncomfortable. I must admit that I would prefer a backrest as I imagine I may be here for some time.

From my log I watch a fox as it creeps through the shadows, skirting the edge of the wood alongside the field. Luckily, tonight I do not have a long wait and soon hear the excited, playful squeaks and squabbles of over-exuberant cubs coming from underground.

Eventually three badger cubs appear in good light. It is entertaining to watch them first scratch, then scrabble about, biting and chasing each other. So I am a little disappointed when, after a few minutes, they move off as a group and soon disappear into the newly forming bracken. There is an enormous amount of noise coming from the cubs but I can see nothing of the action taking place. Then the commotion fades away, and I think that is it for the night.

I'm pondering whether to slip away now that it is quiet, so as not to disturb any more of the sett's occupants, when the sounds of the cubs suddenly grow louder and more boisterous.

Rolling and play-fighting, the three head straight for me, flattening the young bracken. In a flash the leading cub takes a quick glance back at his pursuers, leaping on to the very log I am sitting on, only inches away from me; he realizes something is different and stops in a sitting position like a well-trained dog. Cub number two glances back, chattering in glee at the game, still unaware the leader has stopped – and then crashes into his motionless playmate. Cub one is almost driven into me with the impact; the third and smallest cub attempts to stop but it, too, slides into the others. By now the first two cubs are practically on my lap. As cub three collides he is so close I can hear the noise of his lungs empty out as I am hit in the face by bad badger breath.

First turtle dove of the year. This migrant is a lot smaller than the common wood pigeon that frequents my woods, but is roughly the size of the garden collared dove. Its call is always welcoming, recognizable by its sleepy, almost purring, sound. This bird appears to favour thickets of birch and willow to nest and rear its young, although I have seen one pair successfully nest high in the crown of a mature Douglas fir.

A large brown butterfly, fast and erratic in flight, races past me on a warm wind. I follow its exhausting progress through my binoculars, and how it does not collide with anything is a mystery, for it flies as though drunk. When it finally settles I see that it is a favourite of mine, a butterfly with a restless soul: the painted lady. It's a huge insect, which I have been told emerges from the dry lands of North Africa, migrating north across Europe to England. As with most of the brown/tan butterflies, it is not until they settle and you can study them that you see them in their full glory. Far from dull, their wings support an array of dark bars and creamy spots.

I've had a busy morning and decide on an easier afternoon, checking on future ride-edge work. I look to the sky to see if I need to take a coat as I will be some distance from the truck if it teems down. The sky is a milky green with streaks of grey, but the air is still warm. I decide against the coat.

I'm taking a short cut across a damp patch of mire when the wind behind me blows up in a sudden strong gust. At first I think it is the sound of a vehicle coming, and I even look behind me. It is the type of wind that builds up, passing over your head in the tops of the pine, screeching like a train. Another gust is approaching, and I can hear it long before I feel it. The blast releases the scent of the pines, which hovers on the wind like an unseen phantom. I cannot help myself and have to stop and listen, breathing in the fresh aroma of warm pine that sweeps around me.

The caws of a crow draw my thoughts away. I glance up to the sound, high in the sky. At times the noise is drowned out by the constant murmur of the wind in the pines. Flying lower, the crow is joined by its mate and the pair drop low in a dizzy dive. They are obviously chasing something, and when they pass me at head level I see the familiar shape of a tawny owl, with its rounded wings. It does its best to lose its antagonists. Bobbing and swerving, the owl heads over some young pine. While one crow carries on the chase, the other soars skywards, then suddenly and violently stoops at the tawny; the owl crumples like an airborne mass of feathers, the force pushing the bird deep into the pine tops, causing a massive burst of pine pollen.

Incredible as it may seem, the owl bounces off the tops of the individual trees and, while still in flight, regains its balance and escapes the crows in the pollen screen.

Without even looking at the bedside clock I know it's early when I wake up. The unseasonably warm air has roused me several times during the night, making me kick the last remaining sheet off my body.

It is still dark outside yet I have awoken alert and aware. Lying still in bed I listen to the final fading hoots of the tawny owls before they retire. The rookery is fully awake, though, its inhabitants uttering their constant droning calls that familiarity almost drowns out. In between the occasional departing calls of the owls I can just make out the shrill twittering of the swallows out hawking in the semi-dark. I leave the house without breakfast, and load the dogs into the truck in the half-light. Driving out of the village I surprise a trio of fallow prickets knee-deep in the damp corn, so I slow the truck to get a better look, and they, uncharacteristically, just stand their ground and stare back. It crosses my mind how quiet they all are, for if it was winter, especially at culling time, I would have glimpsed only their fleeing hooves.

On the ridge of the hill the new morning sky catches my eye. Swinging the truck into a farm gateway I pull over. From this position I have great panoramic views stretching across the valley. In the east a small red dot appears, gradually changing into a thin red horizontal line, like the switching-off of an old television set. The line thickens, seeping around the outline of two cumulus vapour clouds that are growing in size. Below, the valley is still bathed in a light grey-blue haze like bonfire smoke, but above the sky is changing with every ticking second. The red line flickering around the clouds thickens, forcing its way through the canvas, and suddenly haemorrhages around the cloud's silhouette, dispersing sunlight and illuminating the sky: daylight has suddenly arrived.

On the face of the down next to me a lapwing with its unmistakable cry harasses a large raven diving at it from above, driving the raven earthward and forcing it to stoop. The raven folds its wings as though struck, uttering at the lapwing a loud hoarse croak of annoyance. Just as it seems the raven will hit the ground, it swoops skywards with great speed, regaining its poise and position. I watch as it flies slow and low over the ground, unconcerned, and alights on a fence post, much to the frustration of the broad-winged peewit flitting through the air near by. The raven sits quietly and observes, waiting for the ground-nesting bird to land; if the raven identifies where the peewit's nest is it will move in to steal the eggs or chicks.

On the down, patches of yellow within the blanket of green sway, cowslips bowing in unison in the breeze. Peering over a large dock leaf, a young rabbit stares at me until a walking rook passes too close, sending the rabbit scurrying to its burrow.

The lateral lines of the landscape interest me; from inside my moving truck I can only glimpse the views over and through gaps in the hedge. From this position the scenery looks like a picture of straight lines produced by the paint brush of some giant artist. Perfect parallel lines of browns, greens and yellows upon sloping gradients; and rising seams of freshly rotavated ground cresting the summit where only a lone distant tree or copse breaks the divide between earth and sky.

Overhead the twitter of goldfinch and the rising song of the lark.

A bad day, beginning with a phone call from a dog walker who has stumbled on an injured deer that apparently got itself caught in a fence.

I'm glad I still get a pang in the stomach and feel pity for a trapped or injured wild creature. It's all too easy to become toughened in this job, although at times you have to harden your heart for an unpleasant task.

No wild animal takes pleasure in having a human near by, no matter how good-willed the person might be. It is in a deer's nature to flee; it will stress and panic easily when made immobile or contained. When you are called to an injured deer you have to give thought to your own safety as well. No deer will intentionally hurt you, but its flailing legs and antlers can be a real danger.

Approaching the deer downwind, I hope to have a look at him first, but the fallow pricket senses I am there and lurches away from the fence and the two top strands of wire that hold him. With that slight movement I can see that one leg has been pulled out of its joint – how long it has been held here I can't tell – and that the other rear leg has bald patches on it, sometimes a sign that it has been trapped for some time. It would be senseless to even attempt to free it.

After dispatching the poor creature, I inspect the legs, especially near the bald areas; it comes as little surprise that when I skin that part I find bruising and dog-teeth rip marks deep in the flesh. Skinning a deer can reveal many wounds, such as tooth punctures and bruising, that would go undetected otherwise. Chances are the deer has been chased until near exhaustion, reducing its ability to clear such a lethal fence.

Start early this morning but slip up by choosing the wrong high seat to sit in for the first rays of light. When I leave home the weather looks clear and the stars tell of a fair morning. It is only when I descend into the vale that the fog becomes tricky, hanging low and protesting against the illumination of my headlights.

A barn owl appears out of the gloom. I catch sight of it in my side lights as it crashs on to the grassy verge. Luckily I miss it; but it was merely doing what all good barn owls do when hunting. First the silent approach and then the plunge, totally disregarding any traffic. Many barn owls lose their lives hunting that way.

As I arrive at my seat, only the tawny owls are calling to keep me company. Nothing moves. A light wind occasionally rises, rolling the fog away, then falls, letting the

fog flood back in circling motions, obscuring and distort-
ing features and distance. Water droplets from the branches
above me direct themselves to exactly the same spot on
my trousers time and time again. No matter how I twist
my body in the seat their aim is perfect. After two hours
of this torture they finally drive me down.

Hoping the view will be clearer out of the valley,
I make the slow climb to the high point in the wood. I
know the cover is denser there but at least I have more
chance of spotting something than if I stay put. Reaching
the top ride I find good views across the fields. The field
edge is definitely worth exploring, although I know that
being higher up means I will be limited for a safe background if a shot presents itself. When rifle shooting you
always need a backstop. Even if you hit a deer the bullet
will continue its course. Trees are not a backstop; you
must always be able to see where the bullet will finally
end up.

Picking a branch off the ride, I toss it to one side, not
attempting to be quiet. No one is more surprised than
me when I spot two roe deer ahead at about eighty metres.
I inch myself to the edge of the ride, then half crawl and
half slide into a narrow ditch. In such a position I realize
I have no chance of a shot but I decide to stay regardless,
to observe and gather information for another day.

Placing the rifle at my side I glass the two does, one
of which looks heavily pregnant. Watching as they eat

keeps me amused until a crow calls out an alarm and circles low overhead, at the same time as a blackbird raises its voice. Rolling on my back I must have missed the crow's departure, although the blackbird is still very vocal. I rolled back just in time to see a fox step out about fifty metres away – so that was what all the noise was about.

Two does and a fox together on the very same ride!

The deer stand their ground; the fox stops in his tracks, and as he turns his head towards them I imagine him saying, 'Morning, ladies.' After looking them up and down, the fox trots down the ride to the left, towards me. I huddle lower in the ditch, hugging the ground, and slowly put down my binoculars. The fox trots on, oblivious of my presence, for the wind is perfect for me. Like a stone I keep my position, watching him pass me within two feet; I move only my eyes, keeping my head fixed. We are almost face to face and, at this point, out of the corner of my eye, I see that he is carrying a mouse, very much alive, its tiny tail curling out of the corner of his closed jaws.

Nature has no fixed date for when spring ends and summer begins, and plants and creatures can sometimes get mixed up, delayed and left behind in the ever advancing season. I've watched leaves unfurl unusually quickly from tightly wrapped dark cloaks into the most attractive fresh-skinned greenery with vast variation of colour and texture, size and shape, evolving as uniquely as any snowflake.

At this time of year the downlands take on a new shape, with individual trees and areas of scrub lending the landscape an almost parklike appearance. Viewed from a distance such images mimic the artificial, clustered scenery of a child's train set. With a late spring, nature accelerates, but while some trees are heavy in flower others can remain almost hidden. Bare and skeletal, some trees struggle to regrow this season's dress, while hourly changes around them threaten to engulf them in mass cellulose. Around the field edges and within the road hedges the hawthorns flower like a dusting of snow. May blossom exhibits petals of sheer beauty. In the wind, unseen, pollen flies: delicate, sweet and pungent.

Candles of erect blossom ring the outline of the chestnut, while birch leaves are at their best in the spring, with those fresh green tones that no artist's paintbrush can capture. Like a cottage-garden border the road edges overflow as masses of cow parsley tumbles into the narrow roads, while white umbellifers dominate and expand the verges. Flower heads of pink campion extend upright and thrusting, attempting to be noticed among the white waves.

The battle of the seasons carries on hidden within the depths of a roadside hedge, where bryony weaves itself, snakelike, using its tendrils to climb the lifeless broken dry stems of last year's growth, seeking the light in the higher branches above. The blue dart of the swallow swoops across the road, cresting the hedge and skimming the bright yellow field of rape. The rape field appears sunlit even in cloud. It always appears to me to attract any shaft of light, extracting and reflecting the light back to the sky even on the dullest of days.

Today the sky is like a distant seascape, with clouds as white horses. The sun is a clear, colourless perfect disk, hiding behind a transparent cloud. On a small group of colliding clouds a celestial red stain appears. Liquid and flowing, it soon encircles the golden rim of the group, the blend now resembling stained glass. Forever moving, the clouds tumble off some invisible edge before being drawn involuntarily towards a massive formation, dark and threatening. The stain continues to expand, racing fluidly over the outer edge of the clouds like blood on snow, quickly absorbed by the ice crystals, then dissipating.

Walking today in the glade, I notice a rapid movement in the tall grasses and bluebells in front, and instantly glass the area.

What I witness I have never seen before: a pair of foxes are attempting to steal a young roe from its mother. The kid is very young, possibly only hours old. The foxes take it in turns to attack the kid, and as the doe butts one of the agitators the other nips in, attempting a snatch.

It seems to last a long time: a pantomime of attacks and lunges, with both foxes then repelled in a series of violent head butts to the body. This is the first time I have seen a doe so violent, so vicious. At one point in the saga, when the kid is nipped and bleating in pain and fear, the doe actually changes form, standing up on her hind legs and flailing and slashing with her front hooves. Like a crazed stallion she tramples one of the pair. Fur flies, the fox rolls into a ball, shrinking. The doe is intent on killing: she slashes at them again, then gives chase to the larger fox, leaving the kid unguarded. The smaller fox sees its opportunity, dashing in and grabbing the kid by the back leg.

I think it's all over, until the kid cries out. Then there is a snorting sound, and the mother is back. The wild savagery of the defence takes the smaller fox by surprise; the doe becomes a vision of unbridled fury, slashing, butting, trampling, driving the fox into the earth. No sanctuary can be found from the onslaught: the smaller fox releases the kid, and half running, half rolling, is pursued relentlessly back out of my sight and into the sea of bluebells. That is, until the doe finally remembers her kid. She suddenly appears, eyes wide, mouth open, and in mid-stride turns back to her shaken but unharmed baby. My mouth is dry and I let my binoculars fall into place on my chest. For me, it is as though time has stood still.

Today I am checking a restock site when I flush my first nightjar of the year. Nightjars visit most of my woods regularly, breeding and nesting within the heather and molinia grasses. They are magical birds, favouring the twilight hour. I love seeing and hearing them in the forest on a balmy summer's night, with the smell of the day's heat in your nostrils, the aroma of the pine mingling with the smell of the damp bog myrtle.

Migrating back from Africa, the males arrive first, and you can hear them churring from the special branches they select. The churring is so loud it can be heard from quite a distance. I find the best way to pinpoint their song posts is to cup your ears, so that they act as sound directors, increasing the volume.

The male is easy to sex from the white spots on its wing-tips. Female nightjars favour recently cleared areas, preferring to nest on the ground. The camouflage of both males and females is superb. When they remain motionless in a tree or on the ground their resemblance to dried bracken and leaves makes them practically invisible.

The kew–kew–key sound alerts me to another presence. I have to shield my eyes as I look into the sun and have just about enough time to see the small falcon with its sickle wings disappear across the open mire and into a clump of conifers.

I am lucky enough to have areas of hardwood to look after, as well as large chunks of heathland, interspersed with pine crop, and this is the ideal habitat for another summer migrant, the hobby. As the bird glides with its stiff scythe wings and its black mask and moustache, it resembles a small peregrine.

Hobbies are skilled hunters, taking dragonflies as they skim over the wet heath ponds and pools. My best view of hobbies hunting was when I was tucked up in a hedge once next to a heathland quarry. One minute I had hundreds of sand martins hawking flies low over the field in front of me, and the next, two hobbies dived in among the scattering martins. Both species of birds are extremely agile, but the hobbies managed to steal two martins, removing them from the sky on the wing.

It is only when I sit back in the truck today that I notice my trousers are soaked through to my boxers. It has rained since early morning and my so-called waterproof trousers can only take so much. Having to walk in knee-high, saturated, compacted rush means checking fences is not too clever a choice of job on a wet day, but it has to be done.

The sky looks exhausted, its colour and texture changing. Gone are the new dark, thin clouds, now replaced with grey ones, the same grey that rises like steam from the damp rushes and wet pools. I am wiping my own heated steam off the inside of the windscreen when my phone rings. It surprises me slightly that the message is from a dog walker who has found an injured deer. But I suppose no matter how wet or desolate a wood is, someone will have to walk a dog in it. I find it hard to believe that anyone would be out for pleasure in this type of weather.

Swapping locations takes some time; the dog walker can't wait but will mark the spot where the deer is lying. I know the road they are describing descends into a poorly made-up cart track. I unload my equipment but leave the steaming dogs in the truck.

The weather improves on the journey, with slices of welcoming, warm shafts of sun appearing. It is late afternoon, with the promise of a quiet evening. I soon recover the marker the dog walker has recently planted on the hazel bush. After loading the rifle I push my way through, around a big hazel mock, and once inside I find myself in a small clearing. The roe buck has tucked himself well into a patch of blackthorn. How the dog walker had found him I can't imagine, as it is well off any track, unless the dog was off the lead and hunting through this scrub.

I move closer, rifle at the ready, but the breathing of the buck tells me his life is ebbing away. His eyes meet mine, but there is no fear. He hardly even lifts his head – he is ready to give up the struggle for life. With pity, I find myself murmur something to him, reassuring him that it will all be over shortly.

Afterwards I drag him from under the thorn. I put gloves on and examine the carcass. The marks to his leg are fresh and I put them down to the dog that found him this morning in torrential rain, out of sight of its owner. But the bites did not mortally injure the buck. After partially skinning him I find two holes. Neither has been caused by a bullet, but by an antler. The fresh scarring is another indicator of the battle, and the bruising is horrific. It must have been one hell of a fight – who knows what the other buck looks like.

It's quite rare to find an injured wild buck or stag after a fight. I've found only two in all the years I've worked in the woods. In a deer park where you get 'emparked' or 'enclosed' deer, it's different. Fallow, especially, are relentless at seeking out and pursuing injured or sick deer and will literally beat them to death. This I have seen many times.

June

Some things in nature are easily explained away and some things are not. One incident in particular has puzzled me, along with several experts in the field. But, incredible as it may seem, I do have a witness who can verify the following event.

I have a morning appointment one day with a contractor to discuss his future working procedure within a particular block of woodland. Being a bit of a misty, drizzly day, it seems idiotic for us both to stand in the wet and talk, so I manoeuvre my truck next to his and wind the window down so we can talk in the comfort of our cabs.

We are well into our conversation when a female jogger in Lycra shorts emerges from the mist, heading up a slight incline towards the trucks. Her long ponytail flicks from side to side with every footfall, and as she reaches the crest of the ride it is describing circles high in the air. Just then a buzzard, with talons out, swoops down at her head. She ducks just in time and the bird misses, continuing its flight passage into the wood edge.

Both the contractor and I look at each other and

mouth the words 'Did you see that?' Then, as we look back at the woman, the bird dives again, and this time she has to bend lower to avoid being struck. We are out of our trucks and running towards the woman, who grins widely and does not seem either surprised or worried. When we reach her she stops, laughs and, catching her breath, says, 'Funny, that happened to me yesterday!'

After I've finished the business with the contractor I timidly look around the location where the buzzard attacked. Although I check for a nest site locally, I find nothing. A hungry buzzard may make a mistake once, but twice is surprising. I can only think that the adult bird had mistaken the jogger's hair for some sort of prey. Another mystery in nature known only to wildlife itself, with man, as always, left in the dark.

June is the peak time for squirrel damage, when, for reasons known only to them, they cannot resist stripping the bark off the good-quality trees. The hoppers, full of poisoned wheat meant to entice the animals away from the trees, are completely ignored. In a situation like this, the best course of action is to wait for the culprits and shoot them in the act, although June is a difficult month for that as there is so much vegetation on the ground and cover in the treetops.

I park the truck a good distance from the beech that

I am going to protect. The shaded, rich green canopy gives little relief from the heat of the sun's rays, and the air is heavy and warm.

Movement towards the crop has to be slow, and all noise kept to a minimum. I avoid walking in the dappled sunlight that filters down through the treetops, for squirrels have great eyesight and even better hearing. Like the squirrels, I too watch for movement on the dry, crisp forest floor and above within the canopy. In this environment all sound is enhanced: you can hear a leaf turned over by a mouse.

The forest floor has lost its damp earthy smell, which has been replaced by the scent of warm air rising. As I pass an insignificant ash that is covered in ivy from the trunk upwards, well into the high branches, a wren scuttles from within. It scolds my intrusion, and its young shriek their annoyance at the disturbance from inside the dense, waxy interior.

What seems like a million hoverflies hum above and all around. Occasionally a large fly zooms in at head level to inspect me, its wing-beats sounding like a fire engine getting louder and louder, then fading just as fast. Even when the fly has passed, its hum still bounces around in my head and resounds in my ears.

Finding a stump with good vision all around, I sit with the shotgun across my waist. Chaffinches and robins sing all about, and in the distance a cock pheasant calls out.

Wood pigeons have wing-beating fights high in the roof of green, but, although I hear them, I can see little of the activity.

A nuthatch repeats its alarm call, and it's then I notice a leafy branch twist. High in the canopy, small discarded pieces of bark fall from above, and I know the meaning of that familiar chip-chip sound. I wait for what seems ages. First I see its tail, then the reddish flanks are exposed. I shoot and send it tumbling to the ground with a dry, dusty thump. The foliage erupts as another squirrel hugs the contours of the beech branches, again racing away at speed; I shoot, but miss. I hastily leave my seat and follow the moving branches. It's soon two trees away, and running has never been my strong point. Stopping abruptly, I aim at the point the squirrel is heading towards and, as it leaps, I shoot. This time I win the race.

Finding a convenient spot I resume my wait for another half-hour, passing the time by watching the sunlight through the stems of the plantation beech. Distant trunks appear dark, but closer up they have the grey colour of elephant hide. After three hours of waiting I have accounted for eight squirrels.

From my viewpoint I can see dark, slow-moving thunderclouds heading my way, and after the first streak of lightning rakes the sky in the distance, I decide it's time to leave.

I pride myself on having no, or minimal, harm done to the trees I am protecting against squirrels. At the end of a season it's frustrating when all your resources are in position but you are still getting small pockets of damage; when the hopper sits unused with no prebait or poison being taken. When you get a few squirrels chewing bark over a period of time they can cause a huge amount of injury to the trees.

By mid-afternoon I have almost finished my rounds of filling up the hoppers and prebaiting the tables with maize to attract the squirrels. I lock the barrier, return to my truck, and just as I open the door I spy a squirrel on the track – luckily it hasn't seen either me or the truck.

I lean into the vehicle and retrieve my shotgun from the gun cabinet behind my seat, while still watching the grey bundle that is galloping towards me. Finding my cartridges is not so easy as I have a mixture of sizes in my box. I have to take my eyes off the squirrel while searching for the correct cartridge, and, when I look up again, the squirrel is gone.

The swoosh of the hazel branches just off the track gives away the creature's position. I stalk quickly towards the bush. I am tempted to shoot the swaying branches, but with no clear target I resist the urge. I glimpse some grey high in the bush and raise the gun in preparation, but as I do the activity stops. Like a statue I stand on the track, knowing I am being peered at from within the dense screen of branches.

On the shaded ride where I wait, the midges start their irritating nipping around my eyes and ears. I am glad when a sudden afternoon breeze picks up. By now I have been standing for three quarters of an hour, though it feels a lot longer. The squirrel starts scolding me from deep inside the greenery. It is close, but in the thick rustling vegetation it might as well be a mile away.

The wind pushes the branches around and up and down, and occasionally I can glimpse inside the large hazel stand. I have almost given up when the scolding ends. I glance at my watch, allow for a couple more minutes of waiting, and then I see him creeping slowly through the branches in the direction of a large ivy-covered oak. He pauses, the wind dies and my view has gone again. I wait in anticipation – as soon as I see grey I can shoot, I tell myself.

A breeze once again parts the canopied limbs of the hazel bush, the squirrel comes into view and at once I raise the barrels and aim. The moment has arrived. But experience stops me from firing, for immediately behind the squirrel are two stocky, downy objects of grey. Four large black eyes stare at me from within the bush, then disappear again as the wind picks up, lifting the branch up and down like a yo-yo. The juvenile tawny owlets look glued to the branch, which disappears down into the greenery then bobs up again, reappearing, dancing to the rhythm of the wind.

I feel relief and vindication that I did not take a shot at the movement and sound of the scolding squirrel. If I had, there's a strong possibility that I could have shot the two unseen chicks. I cuss the squirrel, put the gun away, pat myself on the back and drive on to finish the last of my trap lines.

When I see the long elegant glides of a white admiral sweeping over the ride, I know my conservation ride work is going right. The white admiral is a lover of both dappled shade and full sun. I have seen this swift but graceful butterfly sunning itself on the leaves of a bramble or circling high in the canopy with slow but strong wing-beats. The female finds her way into the shadier areas of the wood and searches out dangling lengths of honeysuckle on which to lay her eggs. I always believe if you have honeysuckle on any shrub in the wood it is a bonus; many insects and mammals make use of the leaf, the flower and the pollen.

The butterfly that finally emerges from the chrysalis is not only handsome in colour and markings but also dainty in flight. On the wind this large butterfly appears black and white, but if you get the chance to view it up close you can make out the white bands and darker spots that distinguish it as a remarkably noble species.

This evening the heat of the day still hangs in pockets in the air that you can feel on your skin and smell in your nostrils. On the breeze I stop to savour the damp, earthy sweet smell of the bog myrtle as a light mist rises from the ground. Around the next bend of the ride, the scent of warm pine bark and heather vapours are carried through the air. As the last rays of the dying, almost full, blood-red sun touch the earth they cast fingers of light that speed across the spiked molinia plumes, then fade into the oncoming dark.

I find a dry sandy bank between heather of two different ages and push my back into a sturdy Scots pine. With the sun gone from the heavens, only diagonal shreds of red remain stretched out in an ever-darkening sky. Stark larch and Corsican pine tops, long established, extend their top limbs into the crimson. The vision looks wild and yet surprisingly natural. Already the shadows and shapes jostle for position for the evening. Shapes become more exaggerated at night, more interesting.

Looking under the branches of the Scots pine where I sit, I see a pine cone, like a beehive with bristles, or a fairy-tale candleholder, its cup held by the tree, steady and firm, a significant part of nature silhouetted against a restless sky.

Overhead I can hear the moaning murmur of a roding woodcock as it crests the pine tops, calling out with a whistle and a croak. Its wings beat the silent air noisily.

With its slow-motion flight it looks as though it is on a string, being pulled through the sky. It disappears into the inky blackness. Its call is still ringing in my ears as it reappears again, following the same pattern across the dusk sky.

On the wet heath mire, near where old trees starved of nutrients and left misshapen stand, the sustained churring song of the nightjar begins. Above me, one bird is already out hunting, hawking over the isolated mire. I watch and listen until almost the last of the dim light disappears from the sky, and make my way back to the truck.

Comhairle Contae
Fhine Gall
Fingal County
Council

Fingal County Libraries
Baldoyle

Customer name: Byrne, Sandra
**Customer ID: **********5715

Items that you have borrowed

Title: A year in the woods : the diary of a forest
ranger
ID: FCL50000367479
Due: 05 June 2024

Title: Enchantment : reawakening wonder in an
exhausted age
ID: FCL30000078729
Due: 05 June 2024

Total items: 2
13/05/2024 11:13
Borrow 3
Overdue 0
Hold requests: 0
Ready for collection: 0

Items that you already have on loan

Title: The Sunday lunch club
ID: FCL3000000132
Due: 05 June 2024

Thank you for using the SelfCheck System.

July

Today the hemp agrimony, brambles and thistles at the edges of the rides are alive with silverwashed fritillary, ringlets, gatekeepers and the occasional white admiral. I can't resist stopping and staring at all the activity. Life is exploding everywhere. The constant buzzing and hum of hoverflies, chirping of grasshoppers, courtship, mating and aerial combats of butterflies all taking place on even the smallest of bramble bushes in every corner of the wood.

I am experimenting with a new type of fence made of plastic, similar to the type used to cordon off roadworks and building sites. This new fence has been ripped by badgers gaining access across their invisible ancient routes. I place some small sticks over the gaps in the fence made by the badgers. I can then check them in a few days; if they've been disturbed this will be an indicator of whether the gaps are used regularly. If so, I can put in a swinging badger gate that old brock will have the strength to open but which excludes any unwanted visitors to the newly planted site.

Too hot to spend indoors. Set the tent up in the garden. Up at 4.00 a.m. stalking – shot roe buck.

Sleep out again, up at 4.00 a.m., still warm enough to go stalking in short sleeves. This morning I can feel the warm packets of air that have been trapped overnight throughout the wood. I can even smell the heat spots.

As I creep, keeping to the shadowy ride edges, I notice a young buck about two years old lying at the bottom of a hemlock tree. It has seen me but stays in its position. I stalk past as though I have not seen it, taking care not to get level with it. Deer get uneasy when you are opposite or level – it seems to alert them to the fact they have been seen or targeted. After stalking past, I prepare myself, turn, stand and shoot. The buck never gets to his feet.

It is time for the monthly dormouse-box check. Three young sparrowhawk fledglings flutter around me as I examine the boxes, their calls similar to those of a lost roe kid. I manage to get glimpses of them only through the dappled shade of the pines. When you reach the tree where you last heard them call, they pause and remain silent.

Whenever you have to lie in wait for a bird or animal in hiding to move or fly, our human nature dictates that we are always the first to lose patience and concentration, never the creature who is trying to avoid detection.

Today I set the alarm clock far too early. I load the dogs and turn the truck off the hill. As I do, large numbers of moths scatter from my headlights.

Above, a flickering light around the base of a dark ribbon of cloud that runs the course of the hill suddenly fires out a streak of summer lightning; the hill and its slopes show themselves to me for a split second and then are plunged back into obscurity. I wind the window down, willing and expecting the thunder, but it doesn't come. The moist, warm morning air gives me a clue to the forthcoming day's weather: expectations of a humid day.

I open the barrier to the wood, scanning the clear fell from the side of the truck. The tops of the small young pine stretch out above a ground mist that hovers over the wet heath. I get the feeling I'm being watched and turn around to see the unmistakable outline of a fox; it stares hard, motionless like everything else on the restock.

The morning light is coming slowly as I drive carefully down the gravel track, looking from side to side and trying to keep myself out of the ditches. Movement catches my eye. I pull over and scan a narrow rack, where a pair of courting roe are unaware that their seasonal love dance is being observed. She stops, he advances. She resumes the chase, he follows.

I reach into the truck, unsleeve the rifle, load and slowly mount it on my sticks. As the pair come into view again, I glass the buck – a reasonable middle age. The sun's crept across the rack, as the panting pair bathe in the light, their coats shining glossy fox-red. I unload the rifle, and the clatter of metal on metal alerts them to my presence. They both stare expectantly. I call to the doe, as though she will understand: 'Don't worry, I won't shoot your lover!'

I don't have much hope of getting a roe buck this morning. The small wood is surrounded by maize on three sides. Deer can become invisible for a good part of the year in this form of cover.

On the outside of the wood, mature unbrashed Douglas firs at head height with dry, sharp, dead branches guard the exterior. On the forest floor dessicated needles on bare ground make sure every step is audible from metres away. In the very centre of this block, a thick band of hazel of various ages surrounded by a wall of rhododendrons defends the interior. The sun has yet to rise.

Creeping on my hands and knees I make it to the second line of trees within the boundary of the field. Brittle, dead branches scrape my face and neck, cobwebs irritate me by fixing their itchy webs across my lips to my ears – each one has to be removed, necessitating extra movement. All this could bring me to the attention of a sly roe buck concerned with not being seen.

Entering a very small glade and trying to make the best of a bad job, I decide to wait. Walking makes too much of a racket. I will wait and allow a better light to develop before giving a call in the hope of attracting a buck. I look at my watch as the first rays of sunlight hit the bark of the tree next to me. It is 5.15 a.m. The red glow slides slowly up the coarse trunk of the Douglas; the light looks like a fire that's been allowed to burn down just before bedtime – a bright crimson encased in a pale yellow halo.

After making such a noisy entrance I decide to let the wood settle down and find its own rhythm again. Squirrels occasionally bend branches around me in the poor light, then release them with a swoosh, like monkeys in a rainforest, in their search for hazelnuts. If you listen to the wood on a very dry, still morning, you can hear many things: squirrels in the canopy cracking hazelnuts, the discarded shells falling to the forest floor; a badger scraping up litter for bedding deep in the rhododendron bush; even mice and shrews moving under the surface of the forest floor, which for them is an ocean of parched leaves and needles. I listen to the high-pitched squeaks of a pair of shrews, fighting only feet from me, yet unseen from where I sit by a large Douglas fir. It always fascinates me how silent mammals can be, and how close they can get to us before we even notice them.

A roe doe, deep in her summer coat of fox red, is just manoeuvring herself under a low branch. As she ducks her head the activity catches my attention. She looks round, alert, in my direction. My rifle is ready, resting on my cross-sticks, my elbow wedged into the gnarled bark of the tree. I half expect a buck to follow, so I peer beyond the doe into the gap in the rhododendrons through which she first entered the glade. Nothing.

From the corner of my eye I study the doe's progress as she passes me, but her body language tells me she is on her own and unaware of my presence. Then the wind changes direction slightly and I hear the click of her hooves as she bounds back to the rhododendrons where she first appeared. After a time the wood falls silent again.

When I glance at my watch it is 5.45 a.m. I pull my deer call from a leg pocket in my trousers, check the time again through habit, then call. The sound is similar to that of a young sparrowhawk. I hope to make the call sound more like a doe on heat – I give two low calls and leave it at that.

Deer can come running to a call, suddenly bursting through the brush, or race straight towards the sound, pinpointing its direction from a good distance away. Or nothing happens. If you don't wait at least fifteen minutes after the call it's not worth making. Half an hour is even better, but human patience quickly wears thin. You start to get fidgety, you swipe at an occasional fly, or lean the rifle against the nearest tree.

I've been here twenty minutes, standing in silence, when I hear the buck, just moments before I see him. It's incredible how alert you suddenly become, and how quickly your senses tune in. An exhausted exhale, almost asthmatic, with an occasional whine, similar to an athlete after a long race, is the only way I can describe the sound of a curious buck searching. This one is oblivious to me, bewitched by the scent on the wind that he pursues with flared nostrils. Judgement of this buck has to be made in seconds, for soon, like the doe, he too will wind me.

He enters the glade swiftly and passes the area I've identified as one suitable for a safe shot. As he weaves his way towards me, I notice another place that the doe passed which would also suffice. Selecting this area with the cross-hairs of the scope I shout to the buck to stop him. The word 'Morning!' has no effect; I call again, this time louder, trying to break his trance. It works. With a confused look on his face he stops, pausing long enough for me to place the shot.

I feel a pang of guilt in the silence after the shot, for finishing him before he had a chance to spread his seed. I respect and love deer but try not to become too sensitive, because if I were to think about the task too much, then I might not want to do it. And I remind myself again that culling plays only a small part in coexistence, in the bond that holds between myself and the deer.

'I bet you know the woods like the back of your hand.' I've had that said to me a few times. There are times when I think I do, but in the woods you are always learning and, just when you start to get cocky, something happens that soon puts you back in your place.

This afternoon I want to transverse an area I hardly frequent: it's too hilly for stalking and the rutted ground makes for miserable walking. All morning I have been collecting my hoppers and loading them into the truck, ready to empty, clean and store them away until next season. Finishing at 2.30 p.m. is an awkward time – too late to start anything new, and with no rifle on board I am not prepared for stalking. I decide the time will be best spent exploring this area; I have seen a very good roe buck near by and want to have a better look if possible.

The region is suitable for nesting raptors, and, with chicks calling, it would be an ideal time to find nest sites that I can map for the future. But now my dogs wind a deer in some bracken, and when I see him I wish I had my rifle. A poor-headed yearling stands only yards away, watching me and the dogs pass. I tip my hat and wish him good day – our paths will meet again.

As I walk further the trees change from softwood to hardwood ash and sycamore. Further in, I find an old boundary consisting of an earthen bank hedge, with mixed hazel and field maple abounding, running the ridge of the bank. I clamber down to a place I have never been to before, pushing myself under a patch of blackthorn.

The ancient boundary hedge finishes on a small ridge. Haloing above this understorey of mature scrub, and towering to the clouds, is a magnificent old beech. I touch its bark, walking around it and feeling the scars that have been inflicted in past years. Standing back I attempt to read an inscription: it gives a name and is signed 'Egypt, 1914'. I run my fingers over the scarring again, wondering how an Egyptian had come across this tree, in a wood in Wiltshire. And what made him carve his name and birthplace?

Around the base of this great specimen are the beds and scrapes where my big buck rests – I have found his home. I expect he's standing unseen, looking down from the ridge, watching my movements through his kingdom. I've heard it said that some wildlife roam in a sweeping radial arc, as if at the end of a lead, always returning to the stake in the centre.

I find it astonishing that animals who, by nature, try to remain elusive to man, such as deer and even fox, can pronounce their presence in a territory so clearly that they are as good as dead if hunted by a person with practised eyes. This instinct to remain in a familiar place, their own domain, can often be their downfall. This buck would be safe from me for a good few years yet, and like all old bucks I will see him only very occasionally, more through chance encounter than hunter's skill.

A large crescent-shaped shadow cast itself slowly across the top of the sunlit down. Looking out from inside my truck on to the hill, every scrubby bush, field edge and boundary fence is clearly lit by the sun. The sky is a heavenly blue interspersed with white woolly clouds: a perfect July day. It looks like it's going to be the first dry day in weeks and I am going to make the most of it.

Time marches on, and the forest never stays the same. Today finds me heading for a site that has just been planted with small trees and where a problem has occurred: a middle-aged buck that I had previously left alone to live his life out here is now browsing heavily on the new young growth of treetops. Looking at the site is like reading an open book: all the signs are here, but I have yet to see him.

In fact I'd spotted the buck only once before, two years ago, at about this time of year, with 1 August fast approaching. I remember our chance meeting at dusk on that occasion. Back then this area was a lonely clear-fell site. The mature trees had only recently been cut and all the lop and top lay spread across the area, smashed and split, completely covering the ground. What were once pine branches festooned in bright green healthy needles now lay dismembered and scattered, turning rusty red, drying up and dying in the day's sun. To a non-forestry person the area might resemble a bombsite. But to the initiated it was another welcome temporary open area for a future nightjar or woodlark to stake its territory and hopefully nest. It was actually my search for nightjars that had first drawn me to the place on the night I met the buck in the gloom of dusk. The site has since healed, and all the brash raked up by a slew and burnt in large heaps. Two years of colonizing vegetation have left their mark on the area, with tall grasses and sharp rushes in the wetter areas and heather and bracken on the dryer slopes. Unfortunately, the middle-aged buck with his appetite for the newly planted trees in the area has now become a problem, which I reluctantly have to deal with.

Within this part of the forest there are two grazing strips that a local farmer uses for his cattle, and I can imagine any rutting buck would make use of such a terrain. Close to the forest boundary is an area of heath, mire and small regenerating pine and birch that is owned by the MOD. The MOD ground and my forest block have masses of invasive, buck-hiding bracken.

It takes several hours to high prune a line of pine that

will give me vision the length of the grazing strip, and, while I am pruning, the mosquitoes are feeding on me. When I finally finish, I push the high seat into place against a semi-mature Scots pine, and tie it off, my hands and ears burning from the insect bites.

When I'm halfway down the seat, I glimpse a pair of antlers gliding through the bracken, behind me in the forest crop. I slip down from the seat quietly and push the bracken away, leaving the two dogs sat at the foot of the seat, snapping at the irritating mosquitoes. Within the bracken I find scrapes in the mossy forest soil in small patches, a sure sign that I am in the buck's home range. At some point our paths will meet. Getting back into the truck is a real joy; I close the windows and spend the next few minutes frantically scratching.

I return with bug spray the same night, but only catch sight of two fast-moving shadows crossing the grazing strip; it looks as though the buck is trying to stop a doe crossing on to the neighbouring ground.

The next two days I am busy with other things, but on the second evening, with the weather cooling, I try again. This time I see only a small fox creeping under the fence off the heath. As the light fades a drizzly rain starts, driving me from my perch. Returning to the truck I put the rifle away, pat the dogs for remaining quiet all night, start the engine and flick the headlights on only to see the buck leaping away into the dark forest crop.

The next day the alarm clock is set extra early, and I yawn all the way to the forest. Deciding to leave the truck a good distance from the seat, I walk to it as quietly as I can. And as I approach I can see the buck already out, sniffing the ground on the strip.

He has not noticed me, but I slink into the crop as I am far too exposed on the field, and I lose my view of him. I make it to the seat, but from my viewpoint I can't see far enough down the field; he is hidden by one small branch, drooping from the the weight of the morning's extra moisture. I call out into the early-morning air using a partially crumpled beech leaf from my coat pocket, but nothing happens.

After waiting ten minutes I convince myself the buck is working away from me rather than towards me. I scan around, then lower myself from the seat. The buck has gone. With the wind in my face I creep along a carpet of moss, following a ride that runs adjacent to the field edge. With every step I half expect the bracken to explode; this is close stalking, almost hand-to-hoof combat.

At the end of the track, half an hour later, I have seen nothing in the field or the crop, although if he were in the high bracken he would have been easy to stalk past.

At ten metres I have a glimpse of antler and then a shoulder; he stops, but with only the forest trees as a backstop I am unable to take the shot due to an unsafe background. He disappears.

Checking my watch I see it is nearly 6.00 a.m., and because of the wind direction I have to take the long route back around the woodland, or he will surely wind me. I slowly approach the seat again and climb up, glad to get away from the mosquitoes that are buzzing in my ears. It is now 7.00 a.m., and he will soon be thinking of going to bed, deep in the sea of bracken.

I keep as still as I can for another ten minutes, letting the forest settle down. Impatience gets the better of me, and my hand feels for the leaf call. I call and ready myself, and then I hear that typical low, wheezing grunt coming from the bracken. I can hear him but still I cannot see him; he remains under cover opposite me, on the MOD ground. The wheezing recedes. He is leaving.

The forest settles again, and I see and hear nothing other than a green woodpecker above me in the pine. Yet another ten minutes pass. I call again as a Dartford warbler sings from a branch of heather. The grunting starts again and I hear the sound of bracken being pushed aside. Then, suddenly, he is under the wire, broadside and still. The cross-hairs find him.

The forest is always changing, and although I take his life for the health of the trees, his old territory will flourish and grow, becoming a future home to many more roe, and perhaps to his own sons too.

August

See a huge caterpillar today on the heather. Long, thick and green. It gives the appearance of having a series of black bands across its body though on closer inspection they are not bands but, rather, small, evenly spaced dark dots with minute lemon-white spots like stars within. I ask a friend about it, and they tell me it's the larva of the emperor moth.

Today I watch a middle-aged roe buck getting amorous with a crippled doe – he is very attentive, and following the hobbling female and sniffing her rear as he traces her every step in and out of some scrub. I also notice in disbelief a male silverwashed fritillary attempting to mate with a meadow brown butterfly.

You would think, after all these years, that I'd have honed my skills by now.

Today I call with my beech leaf, encouraging a buck from a neighbouring piece of scrub to come to me. I position myself for a safe shot in preparation, scraping any dry leaves from the base of the tree so that if I have to step around it for a shot my movements will remain silent. As the beast races towards me across the field I presume that he will enter the wood by going over a ditch and through a well-used deer rack in the bracken.

I set my sticks facing the safest position, with a background in the direction of the gap, and wait. The buck, being young, will instinctively make for this gap, I think – it's their behaviour pattern. Wrong! I hear a minuscule click to my left, and, without moving, I swivel my left eyeball to its outer limit – it encounters a red blur, which I recognize as the fleeing buck. He must have come through the hedge, then passed unseen in front of me behind a screen of green, zeroing in on the sound I had imitated.

I turn slowly, pointing sticks and rifle to my left as the buck moves away. He stops, sensing something, his continual nose-licking a sign that he is unsure of what I am and is searching for scent. He remains motionless, and then with a burst of speed tears off, only to stand still again. Each time he stops he is in an unsafe position, or standing at the wrong angle for me to place the crucial shot. It's frustrating, yet funny, that we are so often made to look out of place in a deer's environment.

Woke up at 4.45 a.m. and dressed in the morning moon-light. Have no breakfast, just a glass of water, then load the dogs in the truck in this wonderful light. I drive past fields of freshly baled straw, huge squares littering the stubble, all shapes looking strange in the moonlight. It is almost magical driving in this type of light, with the full moon large, bright and peeping from behind the ribbons of dark clouds that scoot across the sky. On the wires, silhouetted against this great moon, sits the distinctive form of a tawny owl. My headlights pass him but he does not take flight.

On arrival I check two restock sites, glassing slowly. It's amazing that even with a bright red coat, a doe can manage to hide in the patches of straw-type dry grass that cover the restock site. Only her ears can be seen as I glass for her companion.

The sun is beginning to stretch its rays across the ground, and as I glance up the ride I notice I am being watched. The roe buck is in the centre of the road, unsure of my shape.

I slip slowly behind the truck, grabbing for my rifle, and squeeze my buttalo call. He disappears into the Corsi-can pine and birch, peering out occasionally, but, surprisingly, refrains from barking. I pull the sticks from inside the cab and set them up at the side of the passen-ger door. Placing the rifle within the sticks, I squeeze again on the buttalo. I only call twice, and then I hear the brash snapping as the buck races towards me over the dry forest litter. He appears as a flash of red, breaking cover, pulling up abruptly behind a tree. I pump the buttalo call again; the young buck cannot resist it. Leaping forward, he bounds into the open. I shout at him, and he momentarily stops, long enough for the shot. Looking at my watch, I see it is ten past six. As though I have made an offering, the sun's rays finish creeping over the forest floor, lighting up everything they touch.

The carcass lay in the molinia grass exactly where it was shot, with the morning light flooding on to it. Standing over the buck, with the sun in the east and the full moon still visible too, I feel a habitual pang of guilt, which mars the triumph of the hunt.

Rule number one: when calling, stand in a dense area where you nevertheless have absolute vision in all directions. Stand against a tree or some scrub if possible, and keep in the shadows and out of the sun or flickering light. Only call infrequently and softly. This morning I do all of this, but my entrenched human opinions tell me that the buck will come from a certain direction. Wrong again! The buck sneaks up behind me, with my wind going straight to him. I am lucky to get him. In deer work you are always learning and you can never afford to be smug.

Three hawkmoths in the garden. From June onwards they are visitors to the garden and the woods. You could easily be mistaken and believe that you have seen a hummingbird in Britain. It is, in fact, a moth – the hummingbird hawkmoth.

This migrant visits from Europe and, although only about one and a half inches long, it travels hundreds of miles to get here, like many of the butterflies that spend time in our country. The hawkmoth loves to hover over the head of the honeysuckle, with wing-beats so fast it becomes almost a blur. It zips from flower to flower, but if it stays in one place long enough you will notice its tongue, which it uses to extract the nectar from the plant. This moth is brown and orange in colour, but the tail-end of the insect has black-and-white bars, a bit like a bee. It's quite a hairy beast, but looks as though it's covered in feathers rather than hairs.

Each morning for the last week the house martins and swallows have appeared restless, joining together for a huge gala in the sky. Copying each other in flight appears to be one of their games, chasing and swerving, plummeting and slicing through the increasingly chilly air.

During the day they appear to separate, hunting out small flying insects. They have one particular flight I enjoy watching – the overexaggerated wing-beat flight. It starts slowly, with low-level wing flaps, then there follow amazingly fast wing-beats, accelerating the bird at top speed, only for it to plummet and start the process all over again.

In the morning they all sit on the electric wires in groups of up to a hundred; then together, as though chased from the wire by some invisible predator, they depart in one communal flock, soaring in their squadrons until returning to the same positions on the wires they left.

As I load the dogs in the cool still air, amid the constant coos of the wood pigeon I can also hear the call of my favourite bird, the raven. I am never bored by the sound or sight of this diamond-tailed bird. The cronk of the raven can be heard at a great distance, even in a strong wind that drowns out other birds' voices.

Ravens have a wide range of calls: one sounds like a ball bouncing on the bare floorboards of a stair, finishing with a 'plonk' at the end. Another is similar to the sound of liquid being a poured out of a bottle – that 'glug, glug, glug' noise.

His courtship displays are just as dramatic in their composition, equalling those of any large bird of prey. Occasionally he will turn upside down and glide, with his belly pointing to the sky. Before I put a moderator (silencer) on my rifle, the ravens used to glide overhead at the sound of my rifle shot, recognizing that a shot meant food, as I often leave scraps for them when I gralloch a deer. Being clever and cautious, they would swoop to suitable viewing trees, watching and waiting for me to depart.

Ravens nest early and I have several on my beat. They prefer to nest in large Douglas or larch, as well as using metal trees, i.e., pylons. Being large, powerful, territorial birds, they will protect their nest site, and I have seen pairs of ravens pursue and attack peregrines and buzzards.

The difference between the crow and the raven is their relative size, the raven being a far heavier version of the crow. The raven's throat feathers are long and pointed, making him look like he's got a beard or a mane. There can be no confusion between the raven and the rook, the raven being the larger bird.

The rook also holds a separate suite of coarse calls very different from its larger cousins, the ravens. The adult rook has a grey beak and face feathers, unlike the huge, heavy black bill of the raven. The rook nests in a communal nest site, a rookery, while the raven prefers the solitude of a well-hidden nest.

It's 8.50 a.m. A watery sun lights up corners of the ride side, producing a mosaic of light and shade. Thistle-head seeds, all but expired, hang like wool from a barbed-wire fence. Pale mauve hemp agrimony heads, having fulfilled their cycle, stand abandoned in a dejected cluster, their work done.

On the last of these remaining heads, drenched by an overnight shower, several groups of woodland natives flutter feebly: large numbers of speckled wood, a handful of meadow browns and an old battered silverwash fritillary.

As the morning sun intensifies, a light breeze sweeps the speckled woods halfway up a single beech tree that towers over the mixed scrub and bramble patch. With wings spread open the butterflies bask on heat-retaining beech leaves. Higher up in the top of the beech, a stronger breeze twists the leaves, wrenching and jerking them, displacing the weak. On the very tips of the branches wind-blown foliage flicks from silver to green as undersides are exposed to light against a background canvas of pale blue summer sky.

Open up the barrier today, and on the wooden bar is the larva of the pale tussock moth: a distinctive, fluffy yellow caterpillar with a brownish tuft of hair extending from its rear end, like a tail. Its bright colour is intended to ward off any birds that might be interested in eating it.

September

I finish early this afternoon, so I prepare my personal truck with equipment for an evening's sitting-up on my private stalking ground. I am required to use my own, non-Forestry Commission, equipment – vehicle, rifle, bullets, etc. – when stalking on my own ground. Once there, I reluctantly put on my coat, as I may need it later, and stalk the short distance to my high seat.

The sun is still out and the air warm; placing my rifle on the safety bars to my right, I scan the salt marsh and surrounding fields. To my right, in the bay, I can see small craft with glass glinting in the sunlight and an odd yachtsman with sail aloft tacking in the strong tide, while to the left of me, under an oak tree, a small group of hinds and calves munch noisily on fallen acorns. Snow-white egrets dot the black mud gullies, and on an elderberry bush, which resembles a tree more than a shrub, a scrawny-looking crow savours the bountiful berries.

A flash from across the bay catches my attention – a speedboat returning to the harbour. A mass of seagulls take to the air as the boat passes, but it wasn't the boat that disturbed them from their feeding grounds. Overhead the dark form of an immense bird looms above the panicking flock; the gulls make a meaningless circle in their attempt to escape but the giant bird is not interested in them. Jumpy waders, in an hysteria of flight, explode from the ground, zigzagging across the mudflats in the wake of this menace.

The osprey is unimpressed with all the frenzied nonsense going on below: from its claws hangs a flailing fish that it must have plucked from the estuary waters. I watch as the bird fills the whole lens of my binoculars, passing low over the oak tree that holds my high seat.

Occasional shots boom out across the marsh as duck hunters on their first foray of the season try for a stubble-fed duck. As the sun drops slowly from the sky, I track the progress of a few fishing boats, which are crossing the bay seemingly now with more urgency.

With the sun hidden, the sky changes quickly, gone is the friendly blue, replaced by ever-darkening edges. The estuary changes too: the tidal race has begun, and water is seething, rolling, advancing into dry, cracked gullies. Its invasion of the reed beds is more dramatic, as severe frothy foam is tossed around the reed stems at the edges of the creeks.

Suddenly, as though God has opened the curtains, the sun paints the reed bed with light. It's an unusual sight, although I have seen this happen before: at the last gasp of sunlight the estuary takes on the appearance of an African savannah, the sharp reeds and rushes coloured straw yellow. The strange light whips across the marsh and is gone, and once again I am plunged into the feeling that a new season is arriving.

The deer have sensed that dusk is coming, and I can hear their soft whines. A huge stag is tucked in the reeds to my right, its antlers clean of velvet, blending with the reed spears. Protected by his screen of green, the stag stands stock-still, observing the open expanse of marsh.

From the reed bed, the squelching sounds of hooves sinking into and being sucked out of rich dark marsh mud are quickening; young calves, excited and keen to feed, bleat to their mothers to hurry.

More stags' antlers appear at the line of reeds, but the stags are all reluctant to step out of safety and on to the marsh mudflats. As a small flock of ducks flies over the reed tops just above the antlers, the largest stag steps out. The wind ruffles his black shaggy mane. Standing there, in the gurgling creek, amid the calling waders, he looks somewhat primeval.

After surveying the mudflats for signs of danger and finding none, the stag treads stiffly across the low marsh stubble towards the meadowlands on the shore side. Hinds with calves of various sizes, who dance and skip, race and play, glad to be moving, cross in a procession to the right of me, as I sit trying not to move in my seat.

The day is fading fast and lights are going on in buildings across the water and on the far shore. I can now see buoys in the harbour flashing their warning signals, as a small, poor-quality sika pricket comes out of the reeds to join the parade snaking past my seat. Sika are very acute and will often stop and stare straight at a high seat pitched in the shadow of a tree, so I move as slowly as I can within the confines of my seat.

Watching the pricket journeying towards me, I follow his long swim across the flooded ditch and his jump over a deep black hole. Positioning myself for the shot, I let a group of stags pass. Then, as he runs to catch them up, he pauses before another trot. I was ready!

I drag him back to the shoreline and to my oak tree, as the sky darkens. In the light of the half-moon, I can see that the herd, which scattered at the shot, is now reunited and halfway across to the meadows. It is always a humbling experience to be on the marsh, witnessing the rhythms of this special wilderness.

Above me a wonderful almost full moon, its new light spread before me. Below my high seat a cock pheasant cautiously strides towards me in the deep ruts created by the forwarder tractor that has been hauling out the timber. He steps awkwardly, straddling the large tread marks that are cut deep into the mud, imprints of the tyre. Puddles of static water, held prisoner, lie trapped within the high ridges of the rut. As the pheasant crosses each muddy pool one at a time, its shadow is cast on to the water, following behind its owner in a catch-up game it can never win.

October

I find it hardest to get up in the morning in October, before the clocks go back. I'm always more tired, and the dark mornings add to the problem.

I struggle with the urge to stay in bed for just a few more minutes today. There is no time for breakfast, so I load the dogs and somehow find my way to the wood half asleep. I walk the twenty minutes from the truck to the high seat in the dark, treading carefully and listening to the tawny owls. The first light is approaching as I reach the seat, and in the large recently thinned beech plantation behind me I can see clearly between the grey of the trunks.

It is the first cold dewy morning of the season, and droplets are shed from saturated leaves high above me. The air is still and heavy, with a damp, earthy feel. The stems of the beech shine grey in the pale light. With such wide spacing between each trunk, you can look through at a distance and get a 3-D effect. In front of the seat in the thicket, the scene is different: a land cast of darkness and shadows.

A pigeon alights to the right of me, head height and level. The branch it has chosen to land on is too thin for the bird's weight; it sits as though on a high wire, swaying violently in an attempt to keep its balance. It fails and flies off in an indifferent display, displacing and showering water from the leaves touched in its wake.

A watery, corn-coloured sun brushes the tips of the beech trees below the crown through the damp air. Very slowly the light appears and the shadows slink off into another world, unnoticed.

The rump of a roe buck comes into view, its head down, feeding, searching intently on a small patch of ground. I watch for hour after hour, and it does not move from that spot. When I think the fallow deer have arrived, I am disappointed. What caught my attention was just a pair of wood pigeons, fluttering and playing around a puddle.

I rub the sides of my arms to battle the chill creeping deeper into my bones. No luck this morning – and now it's time for breakfast.

I received a call-out to an unusual situation. In the past, I have seen some strange scenes involving deer and the many horrific ways they seem to find to end their lives. This one is particularly bizarre.

The call comes from a friend, who tells me he's found two deer on his shoot, apparently locked together by their antlers and unable to disentangle them. I play on the side of caution and point out that it is not my ground and he should let the local stalker know. I'm told he's tried several times, but to no avail. I point him in another direction – try the gamekeeper – thinking that will be the end of it, but the phone rings again. Unfortunately the keeper doesn't have any time but he did agree to give me permission to sort out the problem. Sunday afternoon – great!

It doesn't take me too long to locate the deer, for an area of about eight metres square is completely bare of vegetation; around the periphery of this bald area the vegetation is smashed and frayed. I find the pair behind a leafless hazel bush that is stripped of bark, shredded and broken.

I walk with the wind into my face so as not to alarm the pair with my scent, imagining I will see them locked together permanently with their antlers, a sight I have read about but never witnessed. I move slowly in but, as happens in nature, I am spotted straight away.

The larger buck rises, leaping and grunting, with clots of soil being thrown high by his flailing hooves. It appears at first that they are entangled in the hazel bush, which I think is strange. Then I see the reason for this: both bucks have their antlers tangled up with baling twine.

I steady my rifle on my cross-sticks, knowing that I can't, for my own safety, part the bucks. With a deep grunt from one of the pair the bush is ripped, roots and earth, from its moorings, while at the same time the other one is lifted up in the air, a bit like a seal pup being tossed by a great white shark.

I stand in disbelief as I watch this exhausted buck, who has lost all its excess fat, throw what I now realize is the lifeless body of its playmate high into the air. Fear sets in, and the buck drags the corpse around. It shakes its head, frantically trying to discard the dead weight in the low bushes. I have to pick my time for a safe shot, as the buck will not stay still. I have a few seconds when the corpse gets stuck in a V of an ash stool, and then I place my shot.

Both bucks must have been playing with the mass of binder twine when they became entangled. No doubt in panic or exhaustion one broke its neck and the other was left with his unwanted cargo. At least on this call-out I leave knowing I've done the best thing for the deer, and I go home with a clear conscience. Yes, stalkers do have a conscience.

While I am stalking fallow, I move a roe from a thick piece of overstood hazel. The area is isolated by a bank of bramble and wild clematis, not a place you would favour, as it makes any movement extra noisy on approach. I am not surprised to disturb a roe in such an area.

I glass the deer as it hops over the waist-high bramble. After leaping several times and putting some distance between me and it, the deer pauses and glances back.

Between its ears is a poor display of antlers, and my mind automatically files this buck away as one to take out another day. Having already shot two fallow that morning, I allow myself enough time for observance, conditioning myself to learn from the species.

The buck moves slightly, giving me a broadside view, but stops in an unsafe position. I keep my rifle on my shoulder and carry on the viewing I am enjoying. And I learn a lesson: observe 'well'; for my buck is not a buck. Once broadside, I clearly see the anal hair tuft. The deer is actually an antlered doe, and only the third I have ever seen in my life. Although I stalk the whole area throughout that winter, I never see her again.

The weight of rain-drenched leaves has bent a number of branches over across the ride, and the constant dripping of rain droplets after the shower is the only sound I can hear. I sit on my perch, wet and hunched, as the sky turns to a Moscow grey. It feels as though all the action must be happening on the neighbouring land. I haven't seen anything, no movement at all. This happens occasionally, the woods appearing void of all life. But I know the next day will be different. Some way off the triple whistle from a lone sika stag in search of a mate in this unfamiliar territory is almost drowned out by the constant droning of the distant early-morning traffic.

However empty you may think the forest is, though, small dramas still unfold around you if you wait and watch. In front of my seat, a grey squirrel clambers up the trunk of a pine tree in short jerky movements. I watch as he slowly reaches the top. Ten minutes later another squirrel finds its way up the very same pine; halfway up he is faced with the first squirrel hurtling headfirst down the tree. The second squirrel turns and is pursued at great speed with the sound of large chunks of bark being ripped off behind him. With the morning brightening up, it is time to move on.

During my time working with deer, I have witnessed many fights and quarrels. A few end in the death of one of the combatants, but most disagreements usually finish after a mighty shove. With some battles, a mere grunt followed by a half-hearted chase will suffice.

A bad fight, or a good fight, depending on how you want to look at it, is one between two bucks or stags of the same age and size. Such a match requires not only strength but also total concentration and endless stamina from both participants. Both animals become completely bewitched, drawn to this primitive, wild calling.

I am alerted today to one such fight between two prime fallow bucks by the crack and smack of antler on antler, as they both struggle for purchase to keep their feet on the ground. The battle area is only a dot within the landscape, a lonely corner of the forest enveloped by fallen leaves below and a high canopy above, but well known to the deer. Involved in this ancient seasonal ritual is a large black buck struggling with a pale, spotted adversary.

When I first see them they are at stalemate, their antlers intertwined, their mouths wide, gasping and panting. They are both having difficulty breathing, and their sides pound against ever-tighter ribcages. The pair stand tethered in knee-high bramble; they are as one, lit only by a pale autumnal light filtering between drooping beech branches. Transparent leaves, the colour of tarnished coins, look as delicate as rice paper as they twist and whirl in a light wind above them. The breeze separates the expired larch needles from their lacy branch anchors, casting them spiralling to earth; these tiny golden threads soon cover the bramble foliage on which the pair are standing.

Equal pressure is now being exerted by each deer, their thick necks swollen and strained, until the dark buck twists sideways, which means he has all his feet airborne at once. With more flailing and skull-splitting cracks of antlers, the pair dance, joined together, circling an old moss-covered stump with a skirt of fern. Splayed hooves soon snap the upright fern and rip the long tendrils of ground-hugging bramble from the earth.

They are close to me, although neither knows I am here. Their focus is entirely on the other. From behind my tree I can clearly see deep scars on the black buck's neck. Exposed flesh with fur still attached hangs in strips that look like they've been chiselled out, ripped and gouged by sharp tines. Their eyes are bulging now, and their nostrils flaring, and I watch as the pale buck looks to the right for a split second. With this lack of concentration I know the fight is over for him for another season. Looking desperately for an escape route the pale buck backs away, then runs, but he is caught up and, twisting suddenly, he lowers his antlers once more to the ground, facing the full thrust of the black buck's fury. Falling and staggering, his strength drained away, the pale buck turns, exposing for the first time his vulnerable flank, with antlers drawn. The dark buck lunges, but misses. Looking up briefly, the pale one leaps to the side, glancing back for a split second before racing towards the safety of a hazel thicket. Ambitiously, the exhausted dark buck gives chase, partially staggering and attempting to muster up what can best be described as a rather unconvincing groan of dominance.

Samhain. This is the last evening to try for a final cull of roe buck. I have a feeling that nothing will show tonight, but it is too wonderful an evening to stay indoors. The colours of the golden-yellow larch, with that last ray of light, is an unmissable sight, and it is a joy to be out and about, treasuring the seasons.

My truck is coated in a layer of needles that have fallen while I was in my high seat. As I undo the barrier, falling larch needles flicker in the headlights. I can't help but take a long look into the larch tops and at the stars beyond. There was no luck deer-wise, but it was just a great night to be out.

November

At last the rabbit fence is finished and the last of the Christmas trees planted within the enclosure.

Today I check inside the newly fenced area and notice that several trees have had their tops bitten off but none have been eaten. I find indents within the tussocky grass where a rabbit has sat nipping the palatable leaders off during the night.

This morning, after doe stalking, I find time to hunt the dogs through the fenced area in the hope of shooting the culprit that has been nipping the tops off the newly planted Christmas trees. Both dogs work hard, criss-crossing the site in the hope of catching scent. When one of the dogs comes to an abrupt stop and raises its head, I automatically know through her body language that the rabbit is close. The Labrador has stopped almost on point, staring at a small bramble bush, and with a little encour-agement she dives head first, pushing bramble and thorn

away with her nose. Both dogs are excited now, pawing
at a small bare patch inside the bush. I pull the dogs back
and, sitting them down, I discover two small holes.
Returning the dogs to the vehicle, I collect the white jill
ferret out of her wooden box, waking her from her snug
bed of straw. After placing rabbit nets over the two holes
I lower the ferret into the dark entrance of the nearest
one and step back out of sight. The bumping underground starts immediately – dull thumps on damp earth.
All goes quiet, and I hold my breath. Then a grey blur
suddenly bolts into the purse-net. I dive to the mouth of
the hole, clutching the net. I finally have my culprit.

With the fallow rut over by the last week of October, I
decide to check out a stand: an area used by a fallow buck
during the mating season.

A pure-white buck lives at times in the top end of this
block. Having entered the wood from the highest point,
I find a vantage point from which I can survey the beech
woods on the side of the escarpment and down into the
lower valley. Naked branches poke through the diminish-
ing leaf-covered crowns. From a distance they shimmer,
a haze of brown russets and dark bronze.

On reaching the valley floor, I skirt away from the
main track and into a stand of tall mature beech. From
the bottom of a trunk I look up into the underside of

the canopy. The leaf colours and textures from this view are quite different from those I had looking down from above; from below the translucent leaves are a pale green mixed with anaemic yellows.

In the tops high above me, wood pigeons seen from the ground look like balancing shadows. Only the occasional jostling whack of a wing from a disagreement gives their position away. More pigeons arrive, and some settle while others leave with greater urgency. By following a well-worn deer track, I find the start of the stand under a low dark canopy of scrub. The scrub is a mixture of old moss-covered hazel, hawthorn with red berries and a patch of small stunted field maple.

On the edge of the scrub a handful of head-high Douglas fir struggle for existence; all had at one time been very attractive to the resident buck. Fresh sap leaches from newly scored tine marks, the aromatic fir smell strong in the air. Every Douglas has old deep wounds, scarred by thrashing tines on its bark.

Early dark mornings and late nights do not agree with me. It's either one or the other. Lately the evenings seem to arrive much earlier every afternoon. Tonight the scene from the high seat is, to say the least, dismal. An evening painted with several shades of grey, where reference-less cloud drifts down to earth. The secondary line is the ever-thickening mist, its join with the clouds invisible to the eye, a mere crossover of moisture. The cheerless view is not helped by the fact that the site has recently been clear-felled and resembles a silent battlefield.

The mottle of black and white on the trunks of a group of retained birch provides the only welcome relief from the grey all around me. Not far behind me in the tops of the birch, a winter flock of long-tailed tits is busily feeding, their continuous hissing calls a mere background drone. I must have dozed when suddenly – WHOOSH – I wake abruptly to find the air filled with feathers. It is not a herd of swans passing low overhead but a massive flight of pigeons – maybe a thousand – twisting and tumbling, disappearing into the horizon, grey on grey.

I have an early start this morning, and the stars are still out when I undo the kennel door by torchlight. It is clear and frosty, and I am glad that I've covered the truck's windscreen.

As soon as I drive out of my village I enter a vale of fog. I decide it will be safer to sit in a high seat today than stalk in the fog. The rungs of the ladder are covered in a film of ice; I climb the seat in the dark and stare into the morning gloom.

After several minutes I hear the swoosh of wings as a

woodcock alights at the foot of the seat. I strain my eyes to find the shape of the woodcock among a patch of dead bracken no larger than an opened newspaper. Even when I scan the area with my binoculars I still cannot find the bird, although it has probably noticed me. It's times like this you realize how superior animals' and birds' eyes are compared to ours. I must have disturbed it as it flies off into the gloom with a deep annoyed croak.

Overhead in the dark, a small flock of fieldfares lets out a babbled chatter, mocking my hopeless antics. As first light appears the frost starts to retreat and the tree above starts to drip.

The call of nature wakes me up, and with two fingers I prise the material of the curtains aside. Squinting, I peer out at a pirate moon, hanging large and bright in a multi-starlit sky. A few hours later, as I leave the house, I notice that the moon has gone from the sky, but the stars still shine, twinkling high above me.

With my head in the cosmos, I am suddenly taken aback when the outside light flashes on as I pass. The beam lights up my truck, showing beads of water covering the bonnet. Inside the cab is no better, with all the windows uninvitingly steamy and damp. There are rumblings coming from the direction of the kennel, which means the dogs have heard me and are now awake and active. Somewhere in the dark, possibly two fields away, a vixen calls out, pauses, then screams again.

It is still dark as I climb up the ladder into the newly positioned high seat. I sit still, almost bolt upright, moving only to lean the rifle across a secure safety bar, then allowing time for the ripples of my movements to dissipate. High as I am in my seat, I know that, when the light comes, I will have a view of part of the forest that I would never be able to see from the ground. In time I know I will learn a lot about the goings-on of woodland creatures in that part of the forest. All around me individual tawny owls are communicating to each other with long distant hoots and excited kee-wick replies.

In the east a clear, pale yellow sky holds some light, although dark islands of broken cloud race across it, attempting to fill the void. Ribbons of treetops, untouched by the movement of wind, stand stark, framed by the sky. They are of little interest to me until the silhouette of a woodcock, twisted like a wind-blown leaf, skirts the tops. When the woodcock disappears, I drop my gaze below the high seat to the patchwork-quilt blocks of dripping, rain-sodden bracken entangled with bramble in the hope of seeing some deer movement. On my right a steamy grey cloud of mist hovers, rising like bonfire smoke from the ground. Like forest-fire smoke, the mist twists itself through the trees without ever giving away its starting point. These vapours control their own existence,

starting wherever, rising, growing in size, then disappearing as fast and as mysteriously as they are born.

I watch as a ground-hugging fog that is slowly
approaching my seat is swept up into the air; the wind
has awakened. Two winds are at work now: one harassing
the low mists; and the other the clouds high above in a
tempest in the sky. The latter sends streaks of black cloud
racing and regrouping into a mass, ready to do battle
against the ensuing light.

A cackle of fieldfares that have been roosting overnight,
unseen, in a thicket opposite, awake and flush away. They
scatter their winter calls over my head in the new dawn
– a seasonal sound reminding me of wind-blown apples
and snow-threatening skies. At the same time a distant
boom, miles away, sends what must be hundreds of cock
pheasants into a calling frenzy. As the sound of the last
persistent pheasant fades, night inevitably turns to day, as
a shaft of light forces the clouds apart. To celebrate, a
flock of goldfinches, erratic in flight, twitters overhead.
Later eight bullfinches, of which I could see only shape,
not colour, swoop into some scrub behind me.

I glass the glade, the ground mists still knee-high,
hoping to glimpse the shape of a deer, but can find nothing in this damp, dripping world.

Soaring heavenwards a pair of buzzards crosses the
brightening sky, which is now the yellow, milky colour
of a poor-quality egg yolk. On a broken larch top within

a canvas of yellow, a kestrel alights. I watch as it bends its head downwards towards its talons, which hold a small furry blob; with a ripping motion the kestrel tosses the guts of a recently caught vole to the ground. As the bird looks up it notices me and is forced to leave its post. The larch top is left swaying, abandoned against the backdrop of sky. Two green woodpeckers seem to laugh, mocking me for sitting so still, waiting for the expected deer that never appear. I shrug as they laugh again from behind a birch that still retains some of its yellowing leaves.

The sun is higher now and the scene has changed completely: the trees no longer just shapes; the mist a memory; the glade now recognizable.

During the morning I receive a phone call from a member of the public about a deer found tied to a tree. As the message is relayed to me second hand, the exact location of the deer is, to say the least, vague, although I do know which wood it is in. Once there, I find various landmarks that have been indicated during the phone call, but the deer still takes a long time to track down, even with my dogs. It certainly would have made my life a lot easier if the lady could have waited to show me or marked the area.

When I come upon the poor unfortunate creature, I quickly call both dogs to heel and sit them back, well away from the hysterical fallow buck that is leaping in all directions. It circles the tree and with every frantic leap the line that is caught around its antlers shortens, causing the deer to collapse violently to the ground. Its antlers are flailing in all directions, and the closer I get the more stressed it becomes. It is a good-sized fallow buck, and, if I could, I would gladly release him from the nylon cord that binds him. The bare ground around the tree is evidence enough that he has been tethered like this for several days. Not wishing to put myself at risk, or frighten the poor animal any more, I sadly end the struggle with a shot.

It takes two knives to cut the cord from the tree and from the buck's antlers, each knife quickly losing its edge on the thick orange plastic baling twine that has been tripled for strength. The nylon rope and the pieces of fertilizer bags attached to it, known as 'sewelling', is used to raise pheasants off the ground to waiting guns and is suspended across a ride on a series of forked sticks between two beaters. When the pheasants are driven up to the line by the beating team, the sudden pull of the line on their approach frightens the birds into flight, which, in the shooting field, is known as 'flushing'. It is sad that the lengths of sewelling could not have been rolled up by the gamekeeper and stored away until the next shoot day instead of being left in the woods for the deer to find. Most male deer are attracted to anything that swings or moves with the clout of an antler. Once they start playing with it, they find themselves ensnared. The sewelling deer was added to my tally of unusual finds, alongside the deer with the rope ladder attached to its antlers, and the roe doe with the bucket covering her whole head.

Having cleared the last rabbit out of the fenced area that holds the Christmas trees, I see that someone has kicked up the lower part of the fence, possibly to let their dog through, which has allowed rabbits back into the site. I very soon find signs of them: with fresh scraping around the hole entrance and scattered droppings on top of some nearby grass tufts. I ferret the two short holes, but nothing bolts. I fill both holes in with clots of earth and use my Labrador, Liv, to hunt the whole area again after I have checked the perimeter of the fence in a steady rain. But if there is a rabbit somewhere, it is reluctant to move. Then, after practically walking on top of it, Liv flushes a rabbit from a small bramble bush, allowing me a shot. In the short period of time the rabbit has spent within the fence, he has bitten off the tops of fifteen Norway spruce, all in the same row.

Rabbits and hares always leave a tell-tale sign in the form of a clean diagonal cut across the top of a small tree, as if it has been sliced by a sharp knife or cut with scissors. Deer leave a torn, almost ragged, edge due to the lack of top incisors, as they hold, bite and pull at the top or leader.

December

I meet with a farmer who expresses concern over the 'hundreds' of deer he sees in the evening when returning to his farmhouse after a night out. I question him on the 'hundreds' and reduce him down to 'loads'; and then I question the word 'loads'. It eventually becomes apparent that we are talking about five deer, seen regularly, close to the forest boundary, in an area where I have the rights for just the does, and not the bucks.

Normally I carry a portable lightweight high seat on the roof of the truck, which can be put in position almost anywhere at any time. Unfortunately, I do not have it on board right now, so I return, better prepared, that evening.

Before I reach the Douglas fir edge that will give me concealment, I glass a deer feeding close to a crop of turnips, but its antlers give it away as a an out-of-season buck.

When I finally get to the Douglas stand, I settle down and survey the field in the dying light. Two more deer, far away in the gloom, are feeding and walking slowly across the field. After a careful study of them with my binoculars, I can see between their legs a small paintbrush of hair hanging down. Typical: two more bucks, both young.

Finally a doe appears with her young, a buck fawn. She is uneasy and extra alert, and at one point stares in my direction for a long time; I keep as still as a statue. After a series of what can only be described as false bounds, she pauses and glances back at me while standing right on the skyline, which makes her impossible to shoot even if I wanted to. Unknown to her, I would not have shot her anyway, for I never like to shoot a doe with young until at least after Christmas, to give the young more time with their mother. While concentrating on this pair, I don't notice that another doe has appeared in the field. I quickly switch my interest to her, and although it is fairly dark I can see her outline clearly enough to take a safe shot. While loading her in the back of the truck, I re-count in my head the number of deer I have seen that night. It is far from hundreds, but if six is 'loads', then maybe I have seen loads. And when I deduct what I could not shoot, that makes two deer, and one of those is going back to the larder with me.

I turn the heater up in the truck, switch the headlights on and drive through the now heavy rain, thinking it isn't a bad night's work.

The full moon is up there somewhere, swaddled in a blanket of blackness. I search for it when I let the dogs out from the kennels for their bedtime walk. The violent sound of the wind slamming into, and bending, the huge beech tree on the periphery of the garden drowns out all the other night-time sounds. Large droplets of hard-hitting rain urge me and the dogs to our warm nests. Oceanic clouds toss and swirl, mixing and churning the blackness throughout the night, while driving rain hurls itself against the bedroom window.

When I awake just before the alarm clock sounds, it is still raining. I snuggle down lower into the blankets, allowing time for another sudden loud blast to extinguish itself on the windowpanes.

I leave for stalking slightly later than usual, after downing a third cup of tea. I drive to the wood aware of a strange light peeping through the eastern sky and casting a gold horizontal hue, which expands as I travel. Two battleship-sized clouds patrol the sky.

Once I am in the wood the wind is everywhere, changing direction at will, but at least the rain has finally stopped.

Slipping and sliding up a slope between the denuded beech trees, I reach a small open area. Taking advantage of the vista, I pause. After wiping off the condensation from the binocular lens I survey the view below, looking into the wide, steep beech-covered valley. The air that rises from the valley is moist and fresh, with a scent of earth and damp bracken.

From where I am standing a panoramic sky of great distance and depth rolls out in front of me. The gold in the east still holds, but in the west the sky supports an enormous, bright, perfect full moon. The battleships have disappeared, replaced by blue woodsmoke-coloured clouds that pass steadily overhead.

About a hundred metres from where I am admiring the open prairie views of the sky, a hawk-type bird alights from the ground. With strong, exaggerated wing-beats it soon accelerates, climbing high and leaving little chance of identification, before turning sharply in a semicircle and disappearing, swallowed up by the cloud.

The ground is uneven and greasy as I make my way down from the vista to the lower ride. Halfway up the ride I find the spot from where the large bird had risen. On a moss-covered stump lies the half-plucked, half-eaten, still-warm body of a young pigeon. Small, light grey and white feathers, strewn around the outstretched corpse, twist and curl in the wind, scattering in a pattern only nature could design.

Although I expected to view many deer after the wet night we have had, the actual number I see is a lot lower. As usual I could have shot several out-of-season bucks, but I saw only one doe, and she had presented herself in an unsafe position.

Throughout the morning the weather slowly improves, so I extend the stalk, working my way around to the wood edge. In a very grey, wind-burnt, unimproved field, I disturb a small flock of timid fieldfare and redwing that explodes in a resentful flight, arching away to the skyline.

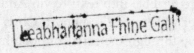

Acknowledgements

I would like to thank Lucy Greig, neighbour and sorceress, who can conjure scribble into text; Kevin Andrews and Robin Elford for welcomed IT support; Chris Yates for pointing the way through the forest of publishing; and, finally, all the friendly staff at Penguin Books, for their support and helpful advice.